JILLIAN DOUGLAS

HOW TO LIVE A GOOD LIFE

A Practical Guide to Cultivating Happiness,
Fulfillment, and Meaning in Everyday Living
(2024)

Contents

Introduction: Mindset Over Matter

Most self-help books often focus on providing assistance but tend to neglect the essence of 'self'. Frequently, they promote the idea of positive thinking as some ancient, mystical remedy that modern society has lost touch with. These guides suggest that by simply asserting your happiness each morning, success will magically follow. However, reality doesn't operate that way; it never has and never will. What these guides consistently overlook is that, for ordinary individuals, maintaining a positive mindset is one of the most challenging tasks. How can you possibly look on the bright side when it seems non-existent, especially in a world where problems like depression, anxiety, and substance abuse are on the rise, and their impact is as significant as that of the Vietnam War on its generation? The cost of living has soared, and the quality of life is steadily declining. Global tensions are mounting, climate change poses a severe threat, and minorities face daily struggles for acceptance.

Not to mention personal adversities like job loss, grieving for a loved one, the end of a relationship, or health issues. There are countless reasons to feel overwhelmed by negativity. So, when life hurls lemons at us, our initial reaction is never, "Time to make lemonade!" Instead, our instincts lead us to seek refuge in resignation and defeat, hoping that when we rise again, the lemons will have retreated.

But ignoring the lemons or repeating daily mantras about how they won't affect us won't help. Even if we possess the tools and desire to turn them into lemonade, it won't stop the lemons from coming our way. It's not problem-solving, nor is it self-improvement. It's still a form of defeat.

So, how can we truly rid our lives of negativity? The honest answer is that it's impossible. The negative aspects of life will always be present. The key is not allowing them to influence or change us. Instead, we must metaphorically grab a baseball bat (or any impactful tool of choice), learn to wield it, and relentlessly beat those persistent lemons into oblivion. This process will be exhausting, messy, and, most importantly, ongoing. Just as we taught ourselves to embrace negativity, we can teach ourselves to adopt a positive outlook. The seven steps outlined in this book are like the ingredients of a delightful positivity cake. However, they won't yield results on their own.

To illustrate, think of baking a real cake. You can gather all the necessary ingredients, carefully measure them, and use your culinary skills, but if your oven doesn't work, the cake will fail. The same principle applies to self-improvement. Engaging in positive thinking for its own sake means little if your mindset remains negative, and that's the root of the issue.

A mindset is your fundamental attitude, one that typically shapes your beliefs and actions. You should focus on changing yourself, not your life or circumstances. Otherwise, you might appear physically healthy, disciplined, and optimistic on the surface, but still go to bed unhappy night after night.

If you're seeking an effortless solution, a magical spell to ward off misfortune, you may not be ready for this book, and it might not be of much help to you. Consider setting it aside until you're prepared to commit to genuine self-transformation.

However, if you're exhausted from feeling the way you do and willing to invest the necessary effort to truly embody positivity, not just think about it, then you're about to embark on a journey to experience the authentic power of positivity.

Chapter 1: Maintenance

Imagine embarking on a lengthy road trip spanning numerous hours, if not days. Your journey progresses smoothly until your car's fuel gauge starts to dip dangerously low. Just ahead, a gas station beckons, but you opt to disregard it, prolonging your fuel reserves recklessly. As you venture further down the road, your vehicle sputters to a halt, the gas tank empty, leaving you stranded. Fortunately, it's not a catastrophic predicament because you have choices. You could walk to the nearest gas station or exert your strength by pushing the car there. Another option is to call for roadside assistance and patiently await rescue, or simply leave it to fate, hoping for a benevolent stranger to lend a hand. Regardless of the path you choose to address your situation, the undeniable truth remains—you're in this predicament due to your irresponsibility in neglecting the gas gauge.

While this analogy effectively conveys the message, it depicts an improbable scenario, as most individuals possess the wisdom to refuel their vehicles when necessary. Regrettably, the same cannot be said for people's self-care habits.

A more fitting analogy would be computers or any electronic device highly valued as a possession. Although the inner workings of computers are intricate, we can simplify their functionality by amalgamating their two primary components: hardware and software.

Hardware encompasses the tangible components such as the computer's motherboard, monitor, tower, keyboard, mouse, and more. Software, on the other hand, encompasses the operating system, coding, and all the applications or programs used on the computer. While most people grasp the distinction between these two aspects, they often forget that one is virtually useless without the other.

Picture a scenario where the software functions impeccably, yet your monitor malfunctions or becomes unresponsive. In such a case, you are unable to access the software. Similarly, if your phone's battery dies or your keyboard fails, you face the same dilemma. Conversely, we have all grappled with the frustration of owning exceptional hardware but encountering issues with incompatible software, memory constraints, or the dreaded updates necessary to maintain our computers' functionality.

Your body and mind share a comparable relationship. Physical and mental well-being are two intertwined aspects of the same coin. It is widely acknowledged (and observed) that one can never truly reach their full potential if one of these aspects is lacking. This is not to imply that individuals with disabilities or psychological disorders cannot experience happiness—they absolutely can. In fact, I will delve into positivity and mental health in more detail later in this book. However, it is undeniable that life presents more hurdles to those with health challenges, whether physical or mental. Where difficulties arise, negativity often follows, and individuals facing such challenges frequently must exert extra effort to discover the silver linings that able-bodied, healthy individuals often take for granted. Regardless of your personal circumstances, here is a question worth pondering: Why do you neglect self-care?

If you happen to be among those individuals who tend to deceive both themselves and me with statements like "I do look after myself, you don't know me!" – let me emphasize that you're clearly not living your optimal life; otherwise, you wouldn't require me to instruct you on how to achieve it.

The majority of us are simply enduring, following the necessary routines to stay alive and avoid medical issues. We consume food, stay hydrated, and rest when possible or when necessary. However, the moment something demands more of us – be it work or even something as trivial as binge-watching an entire series in two days – these fundamental aspects of our survival are the first to be compromised. Consequently, when we wake up feeling terrible in the morning, experience emotional outbursts due to hunger, or endure the pain of exhaustion from insufficient sleep, we ponder why we can't perceive the brighter side of life.

Remember, there is only one of you, and if your physical well-being is deteriorating, your mental and emotional faculties won't function as they should. Therefore, the initial and quite possibly the most crucial step you must take toward embracing a more positive outlook is to prioritize your health. Ensuring self-care is indispensable for achieving a sense of well-being.

Healthy Body, Healthy Mind

I'd like to introduce you to someone named Science, who will assist me in demonstrating the interconnectedness of health and happiness. Trust me when I say that there is a plethora of evidence supporting the link between physical well-being and mental and emotional wellness.

It might not be common knowledge, but every experience you undergo is essentially a chemical reaction occurring in your brain. A prime example of this is the phenomenon of romance. According to Harvard researchers (as cited in "Love and the Brain," 2012), the initial sensation of falling in love is essentially anxiety induced by a surge of cortisol, commonly known as the stress hormone. This explains why you experience those fluttering sensations in your stomach when you encounter or think about someone you are attracted to. The unease, jitteriness, rapid heartbeat, sweaty palms, and breathlessness associated with romantic feelings are essentially your brain's way of preparing for a crisis, as detailed in the Harvard study.

The reason why these sensations feel pleasurable is that cortisol is not the only chemical released in your brain during love. Dopamine, the "feel-good" chemical, is also produced, leading to sensations of euphoria and reward. Additionally, there are noticeable increases in oxytocin, often referred to as the "love hormone," which promotes feelings of satisfaction, safety, and contentment. Another less-known hormone called vasopressin fosters emotional attachment and bonding. Moreover, changes in your brain chemistry essentially shut down the brain's negativity center, making it biologically possible to experience a kind of high from romance. This also elucidates why individuals who are newly in love often seem exceedingly happy.

While love garners the most attention in human responses, the underlying concept of it being a chemical reaction beyond our control applies to all pleasurable experiences. Beyond romance, substances like dopamine, serotonin, oxytocin, and endorphins play pivotal roles in happiness and pleasure. Consequently, increasing the production of these "happy chemicals" can make you a more positive individual. The question then arises: How can you stimulate the production of these chemicals?

You may not find the answer appealing, but it has been right in front of you all along, possibly overlooked or denied. Taking care of yourself through activities like exercise, consuming nutritious food, actively enjoying life, practicing meditation, and ensuring high-quality sleep all enhance your body's capacity to generate and release these feel-good substances.

On the flip side, undesirable and unhealthy habits repress these positive feelings. An illustrative case in point is a study involving animals, where rats were excessively fed junk food. The outcome revealed that their dopamine receptors weakened, necessitating higher quantities of junk food to experience pleasure (O'Callaghan, 2012). This is essentially how addiction to unhealthy substances functions. You might believe you're experiencing happiness, but in reality, your capacity to derive pleasure is diminished. Over time, you find yourself needing more of these detrimental substances to derive even the slightest satisfaction.

Specifically concerning dopamine, a deficiency leads to a range of distressing symptoms (Cadman, 2018). These encompass physical issues like muscle discomfort, reduced appetite, fluctuations in weight, impaired balance, and heightened susceptibility to pneumonia. Yet, the psychological repercussions are profoundly unsettling. An insufficient supply of dopamine can bring about mood swings, feelings of hopelessness, diminished motivation, anxiety, depression, contemplation of suicide, insomnia, delusions, hallucinations, loss of self-awareness and self-esteem, as well as unexplained feelings of sadness and guilt. If this doesn't perfectly illustrate how a healthy body contributes to a healthy mind, then I'm unsure what will.

In certain instances, you may find yourself producing an excess of these beneficial chemicals, which also have detrimental effects on your health, behavior, and mindset. Using dopamine as an example once more, an excess of it can lead to the loss of inhibitions and recklessness. You might become more prone to aggression, reduced empathy, and susceptibility to conditions like Obsessive-Compulsive Disorder (OCD), schizophrenia, paranoia, mania, and addiction.

The principle of moderation applies to each of these happiness-inducing chemicals, and the key to utilizing them effectively and to your advantage is to assist your body in maintaining a balanced production. When your body generates a sufficient quantity of these happiness chemicals, your perspective on life is bound to become more positive.

"Fix Yourself"

Now, we face the challenging aspect of this journey. To maintain a positive outlook, you'll need to balance the levels of beneficial chemicals within your body. These are indeed chemical substances subject to fluctuations, but that shouldn't serve as an excuse to leave your mood, perspective, self-esteem, or mindset to chance. Neglecting self-care in this regard is akin to consciously choosing to wake up feeling sad, disconnected, or negative. While we may not possess complete control over our biological processes, we do have influence.

Let's proceed to the first step: repairing and maintaining yourself. Remember the analogy of a car? When something feels off while driving, your immediate instinct is to identify the issue and take the necessary steps to rectify it. Why? Because operating an unsafe vehicle poses risks, ignoring warning signs could result in a range of problems. At best, your car might break down, leaving you stranded. At worst, you could cause accidents with severe consequences. When something doesn't feel right, you take your car to a mechanic for servicing. Yes, it may cost you money, but far less than dealing with an emergency. It's a responsible action, even if it requires determination and effort.

Similarly, your body requires maintenance, and the extent of repairs and upkeep depends on your current condition. Feeling sluggish occasionally, just as you might experience fatigue, stress, or illness, is entirely normal. I want to emphasize that being happy all the time is unnatural and unhealthy, so don't be too hard on yourself when you're feeling down. However, if you consistently feel low, something is evidently amiss, and it becomes your responsibility to address it. I can't pinpoint precisely what's malfunctioning, but I can help you narrow it down.

Various underlying causes contribute to deficiencies in the happiness chemicals. These include inadequate nutrition, lack of exercise, stress, insufficient sleep, excessive consumption of alcohol and drugs (including caffeine), and smoking, all of which contribute to and prolong insufficient levels of dopamine, serotonin, and oxytocin. But the list doesn't end there. Sometimes, the deficiency stems from pre-existing neurological disorders. It could also result from medical issues such as thyroid problems, obesity, or even side effects or counterreactions to medication. Changes in hormones, such as during puberty, menopause, pregnancy, or gender transitions, can also impact production.

You'll notice that some of these factors are beyond your control, but the majority can be managed. It's reasonable to assume that if you can relate to the factors you can control, the reason behind not addressing them is often procrastination.

I don't say this to criticize. We all have moments of laziness. However, there's a distinction between a day spent in bed and outright neglect of self-care. If your outlook on life appears bleak, it's likely because you're not making an effort to lead a wholesome life. That's not entirely your fault either; we are creatures of convenience. Yet, if you aspire to improve yourself, you'll need to take two crucial steps. Firstly, you must learn to decline things that are detrimental to your well-being. Secondly, you must commit to working on things that promote your well-being. Neither of these tasks will always be enjoyable, but they are essential.

The Habits of Happy People

Don't be surprised if you've encountered everything I'm about to express before, but I must reiterate it nonetheless, just in case you haven't fully grasped the truth and gravity of this counsel.

Successful individuals are those who radiate happiness and positivity, share common routines, lead similar lifestyles, and possess a unified, empowering mindset. Their mindset doesn't shackle them, even when faced with adversity. The reason for this is that prosperous and optimistic people don't solely fixate on the present moment. It's not to suggest that high-achievers cannot appreciate their current circumstances; indeed, they can and do. The distinction lies in their forward-thinking approach, concentrating on outcomes rather than conditions.

It's effortless for someone to advise that exercise is the key to happiness and well-being, but when it boils down to it, exercise can be arduous. It demands time, can become monotonous, can be physically demanding, and, if you lack access to equipment or a safe workout space, it can also be expensive when joining a gym. Not to mention that engaging in exercise often comes with feelings of self-doubt. Maybe you're not witnessing the results as swiftly as anticipated. Perhaps you encounter criticism on social media for daring to share your 'before' photo, and people may not react positively to your appearance. It's plausible that you feel you're not putting in enough effort because you frequently skip sessions due to other commitments, or simply due to laziness or exhaustion. These challenges are situational, yet they can be potent enough to lead you astray until you conclude it's not worth the effort and give up.

That's the full force of negativity. Positivity, conversely, entails affirming to yourself that critics will always exist, but you take pride in your courage to capture yourself even when the photo may not be flattering. Positivity means recognizing that you've invested in a gym membership, so you're determined to derive full value from it. It's a self-reminder that Rome wasn't built in a day, and if you persist through the hardships, you'll eventually attain the physique you desire, witness improvements in your blood pressure and cholesterol, or shed enough weight to feel content with yourself. Positivity grants you the liberty to rest when you genuinely can't push further because you deserve a break, while also motivating yourself to commit just ten minutes a day, regardless of fatigue, to stay on course – the choice is yours. Ultimately, positivity revolves around understanding your desires and choosing to pursue them, irrespective of the negativity your mind whispers during challenging moments.

To underscore the message, positivity is nothing short of dedication. You have the liberty to choose what you're dedicating yourself to self-improvement, health, appearance, or even the determination to maintain a positive outlook during trying times.

Positive individuals don't necessarily have an easier life than others; they are simply more adept at disregarding self-doubt.

Still skeptical? In that case, let me provide you with an example. The names Brian Chesky and Joe Gebbia may not ring a bell, but without a doubt, you're familiar with their creation: Airbnb. These two individuals didn't wake up one morning and decide to revolutionize travel. They were driven to it out of sheer desperation because they couldn't afford their rent and faced eviction. Instead of succumbing to their predicament, they sought a solution. They utilized their available resources – an apartment and an air mattress – and listed them as budget accommodation. Due to its affordability, it gained traction, and it seized the opportunity to transform it into the colossal empire that Airbnb is today, using all four of its hands (Rabang, 2019).

Do you genuinely believe they weren't filled with doubt, stress, fear, and their inner critics telling them that renting an air mattress to travelers was the most absurd idea ever conceived? At one point, they lost so much faith in their idea that they put it on hold, concerned about competing in an oversaturated market. However, they weren't living in the present; they were living three weeks ahead – when their rent was due.

Airbnb is now a multi-billion-dollar company, but their objective wasn't billions of dollars, nor did a fortune drive them. Their immediate concern was paying their rent. They maintained a positive outlook and, as a result, changed the world. I'm fairly certain they'll never have to worry about rent again.

So, how can you commit to positivity? Granted, you may not be in a dire situation that necessitates innovation, but you can still pledge to silence your negativity to achieve what is necessary for a good life. You may not end up a billionaire, but you will have a healthy body, increasing your odds of possessing a healthy, optimistic mind. The following are some non-negotiable items for your to-do list, without excuses.

Get Fit

I understand your hesitation. I don't want to be told that I need to endure physical discomfort to experience well-being either. My primary desire is to write my books and assist people, not to engage in activities like treadmill running, weightlifting, muscle straining, or accidentally injuring myself – all the entertaining mishaps that can occur when you're inexperienced at the gym. Nevertheless, physical exercise genuinely offers advantages for both your physical and mental well-being.

I don't intend to sound like a cliché, but our bodies are truly remarkable, and if you possess some knowledge about biology, you'll comprehend precisely what I mean. Every aspect of our being has a purpose and is finely tuned to operate harmoniously as a unified whole. Throughout much of human history, we mistakenly believed that some parts of our body, such as the appendix, served no function. It's now recognized, however, that the appendix stores beneficial bacteria, contributing to gut health (Warner, 2007). No part of your body functions in isolation. If you were a machine, your brain would serve as the central control unit (and I must add, you'd be an exceptional model!). However, it wouldn't operate through one-way communication. Your brain governs your body, but your body also nourishes your brain. This is why maintaining your body in excellent condition can and will enhance your emotional state and perspective. None of us enjoys being ill, as we function at our best when we're healthy. Think about how even a common cold can spoil your day, even if everything else in your life is fine. Similar to how your computer or car operates more efficiently and smoothly with regular maintenance, you must put in effort to care for yourself. It's the most valuable service you can provide for your body. Looking after yourself ensures that your body functions at its peak for as long as you continue to do so. Moreover, this has a substantial impact not only on your physical health but also on your mental well-being.

Exercise triggers the release of endorphins – the delightful chemicals we previously mentioned. In fact, it's so effective at generating endorphins that it's regarded as a legitimate method for combatting depression (DeNoon, 2008). But it doesn't stop there. Research demonstrates that exercise also prompts the release of dopamine and serotonin, the two major neurotransmitters most likely to influence your mood (Collins, 2012). Furthermore, a less-known animal study suggests that exercise induces the production of oxytocin in the brains of mice, making it probable that similar effects occur in humans (Yüksel et al., 2019). To take it a step further, exercise also reduces stress hormones, specifically adrenaline (associated with anxiety) and the aforementioned cortisol (Harvard Health Publishing, 2018).

Do you comprehend the significance of this? Exercise facilitates the production of all the crucial happiness-inducing substances while mitigating the presence of detrimental hormones responsible for feelings of nervousness, anxiety, or overwhelm. Every detail in this segment carries significance and should not be disregarded if you are earnest about self-improvement. Nevertheless, exercise stands in a league of its own due to its undeniable benefits.

Eat Well

Much like exercising, there are several compelling reasons to commit to maintaining a nutritious and well-balanced diet. The most apparent rationale is that food serves as the body's fuel, and running on empty can lead to irritability. This phenomenon, often humorously referred to as "hangry" by today's youth, has a genuine scientific basis. When you neglect to consume enough food, your body interprets it as a potential threat to your life, triggering survival mechanisms, including heightened aggressiveness (Salis, 2015). It's almost as if your body becomes a bit of a drama queen in such situations!

Although "hanger" may evoke amusement, it is a substantial matter. If you find yourself experiencing significant changes in mood, becoming unusually irritable, or short-tempered, the solution might very well lie in nourishing yourself adequately. Moreover, let's revisit the notion of happiness chemicals because eating plays a role in releasing them too, albeit in an unexpected manner. A captivating study conducted by Finnish researchers discovered that eating releases endorphins. Surprisingly, only indulging in junk food, like pizza in their study, triggers our pleasure response. Healthy food—a nutritional beverage with an equivalent calorie count as the pizza—released more endorphins, yet it failed to induce pleasure responses. The takeaway here is that eating indeed has the power to make us happier, even if it doesn't always offer a physically enjoyable experience (HealthDay, 2017).

Consequently, there are two perspectives to consider. On one hand, if you seek moments of pleasure, it's advisable not to deprive yourself of your favorite indulgences too frequently. Compelling evidence suggests that it's more than just a guilty pleasure; it's something we genuinely relish. On the other hand, healthy food is better for us since it elicits more endorphin release. Over time, sticking to nutritious options proves more effective in enhancing your mood, even if the immediate gratification may not be as pronounced.

Of course, the latter recommendation extends beyond mental well-being because excessive consumption of junk food can have detrimental physiological effects. Maintaining a balanced diet also complements exercise and weight management.

But what precisely constitutes a 'balanced' diet? Honestly, there are countless viewpoints on this matter, making it impossible to provide a definitive answer. Some individuals advocate for extreme diets like the ketogenic diet or intermittent fasting, asserting their potential benefits, while others argue they might be harmful. One person might embrace a vegan dietary approach, while another might opt for a carnivorous route. Decisions regarding what and when to eat require individual research, but one constant remains: any worthwhile diet places significant emphasis on three crucial nutritional components—carbohydrates, healthy fats, and protein. These substances serve as the fundamental building blocks for your body, supplying it with essential energy. Thus, ensuring an adequate and healthful intake of these nutrients is imperative (NIH, 2000).

For this reason, I find the "If It Fits Your Macros" (IIFYM) diet plan to be a promising starting point. The underlying principle is to consume whatever you prefer, whether it's junk food or healthier options, as long as it aligns with your personalized daily macronutrient intake recommendations based on your physical attributes and age (Julson, 2018). It's essential to note that before embarking on any diet, consulting a medical professional is advisable. However, this approach is worth exploring if you are genuinely committed to eating well, managing your weight, or transforming your relationship with food.

Sleep, Damnit

I've observed a recent trend on social media where people are making jokes about serotonin or the lack thereof. This younger generation, known for their excessive coffee consumption, relentless work ethic, and a tendency to overlook the benefits of exercise on mental well-being, often attribute their low serotonin levels to insufficient sleep. However, it's important to note that sleep doesn't directly provide you with serotonin; rather, serotonin plays a pivotal role in facilitating sleep. So, if you're struggling with insomnia or waking up feeling groggy due to poor sleep quality, it's likely that a deficiency in serotonin is the root cause, not the consequence (as discussed in "Settling the debate on serotonin's role in sleep: The brain chemical is necessary to get enough sleep," 2019). This is because serotonin is essential for the production of melatonin, the genuine sleep-inducing hormone (as explained by Raman in 2017).

Now, connecting all these pieces together, it becomes evident that exercise boosts serotonin levels, aiding in the production of melatonin, which, in turn, promotes better sleep. This improved sleep quality can ultimately lead to enhanced mood, mental health, and an overall better quality of life.

Research has shown that insufficient sleep can heighten anxiety and depression, primarily by increasing the production of stress hormones. Furthermore, inadequate sleep can hinder memory retention (as found in a study by Moisse in 2013). Not to mention, it is associated with various health risks, such as impaired cognitive function and an elevated risk of cardiovascular problems and diabetes. In essence, sleep is a vital component of a healthy lifestyle, and it's clear that we need more of it.

Nonetheless, there is a prevailing notion that the quality of sleep is more crucial in regulating one's mood than the quantity of sleep. This notion follows the reasoning that even if you manage to get the recommended eight hours of sleep per night, poor sleep can still leave you feeling fatigued. The primary purpose of sleep is to rejuvenate and reenergize the body. Hence, many believe that the quality of rest holds greater significance than its duration.

What we do know for certain is that sleep deprivation is closely linked to mood disorders and is highly likely to result in irritability, anger, depression, anxiety, and other emotional instabilities (as discussed in "Sleep Quantity vs. Sleep Quality," 2019).

So, if you find yourself not feeling negative but simply in need of better rest, you're not alone in recognizing the importance of quality sleep.

Calm Your Mind

Meditation is a practice that confronts us daily, yet we often overlook its significance. Take a moment to ponder how frequently you gripe about the cacophony, monotony, stress, and the scarcity of time for relaxation. Then, ask yourself why you've been aware of meditation's existence for so long but haven't given it the attention it deserves (unless, of course, you already have, in which case, kudos to you! You're a rare find!).

This technique entails the act of concentrating your mind, essentially training it to attain a state of tranquility, relaxation, and inner peace. Often, it's depicted as something enigmatic or overly artistic, but there is a substantial body of scientific evidence supporting its tangible benefits.

For instance, one study discovered that meditation can boost dopamine levels, elucidating why engaging in this practice leaves us feeling serene and content (Kjaer et al., 2002). An earlier study proposed, with compelling evidence, that meditation also triggers endorphin surges, amplifying the positive sensations that result from calming the mind (Rokade, 2011).

Even more intriguing is the scientific revelation that meditation has the power to essentially rewire your brain for a naturally happier disposition (Lickerman, 2013). When combined with the advantages of maintaining a healthy diet, getting adequate sleep, and regular exercise, meditation becomes a potent tool for transforming into a more optimistic individual.

If you're grappling with altering your mindset, meditation might just be the ideal starting point. It turns out, the hippies were onto something. Who would've imagined?

Do What You Love

For now, my dear companion, science has temporarily receded into the background. But in its absence, allow me to introduce you to another cherished acquaintance of mine – common sense. While ongoing research endeavors aim to substantiate the notion that pursuing one's passions enhances the overall quality of life, we exist in a world deeply entrenched in capitalism, where undisclosed truths are concealed by those in power. Consequently, this valuable insight is relegated to obscurity, and this is where my friend, common sense, steps in.

Recall, if you will, the Finnish food study we discussed a few paragraphs ago, where the simple act of savoring a slice of pizza triggered pleasure responses within the brain. It is self-evident that engaging in activities one enjoys elicits physiological happiness, a phenomenon corroborated by studies on love and the impact of these euphoria-inducing chemicals on our well-being.

Pleasure is a multifaceted concept, akin to an emotion, yet also a sensation. It resides within the realms of physiology and spirituality, and one could argue it possesses psychological facets as well. What we can assert with confidence is that, much like nearly everything else, pleasure is fundamentally chemical, with endorphins serving as its driving force.

However, in contrast to serotonin, oxytocin, and dopamine, which require specific and often arduous circumstances for their production (such as exercise), pleasure is an entity readily accessible in various facets of life. Barring psychiatric conditions that impede the activation of pleasure receptors, the reality is that one wields considerable agency over their own happiness.

Listening to a beloved song, relishing delectable cuisine, spending cherished moments with loved ones, immersing oneself in the thrill of a captivating book, or showering one's pet with affectionate kisses on their plump belly all evoke a sense of well-being. So, why not invest more effort in pursuing these moments of elation?

Many of us bemoan the scarcity of time or energy, attributing it to our bustling lives or external constraints that thwart our desires. We must labor, study, and engage in mundane tasks like chores and taxes. However, this is precisely why we ought to prioritize endeavors that extend beyond these obligations. Not to the extent of neglecting our essential responsibilities, but rather to elevate the pursuit of enjoyment to a similarly crucial status.

If we can spare moments for procrastination, surely we can allocate time to express our admiration to friends or commence work on that long-awaited book. We can plan a getaway or, in dire circumstances, reward ourselves with a piece of chocolate or a comical video.

Becoming happy is not an intricate endeavor; it merely requires practice. The more diligently we cultivate it, the greater our happiness shall burgeon, and the more radiant our outlook on life shall become.

Know When to Quit

At last, let's delve into the realm of common sense once more. It's high time to confront some unfavorable habits you've picked up along the way. It's impractical to tackle every conceivable vice, so I'll focus on those that directly impact your well-being.

One glaring example is smoking. It wreaks havoc on both your lungs and the environment, not to mention it's a costly, detrimental, and odorous addiction. However, attempting to persuade a smoker of this truth often proves futile. They're well aware of the harms, yet they remain indifferent because cigarettes manipulate their dopamine receptors, inducing a false sense of happiness and eventual addiction. What many smokers fail to grasp is that their habit could be a contributing factor to, or exacerbation of, depression (McCoy, 2012).

Substance abuse, too, disrupts your brain's delicate chemistry (as elucidated in "Drugs and the Brain," 2018). While the effects of narcotics and other substances may mimic natural brain receptor activation, they are inherently abnormal and gradually deteriorate neural communications.

Caution is paramount. An occasional drink poses no issue, but excessive alcohol consumption is cause for concern. It becomes even more problematic when you consider how certain substances, like alcohol, appear to alter your personality or reasoning. You might become more belligerent, emotionally unstable, or even sink into a state of despondency.

The imperative lies in shedding these detrimental habits, thereby granting your brain the capacity to focus on the positive aspects of life. Whether it's quitting smoking, curbing alcohol intake, managing food cravings, or conquering nervous behaviors such as nail biting or teeth grinding, these changes can significantly alter your perspective on life. These habits often serve as safety nets, but in the end, they weigh you down.

Enhancing oneself pays dividends in the long run, and sometimes, the initial step involves acknowledging your less desirable traits and then actively working on self-improvement. Moreover, you'll experience a tangible sense of well-being and self-acceptance when your mind is clear, and your body is no longer entangled in dependencies on detrimental substances.

Tips and Tricks to Better Yourself

As previously mentioned, accomplishing each of these tasks - engaging in regular exercise, maintaining a healthy diet, ensuring adequate sleep, achieving mental tranquility, carving out personal time, and relinquishing detrimental habits - is more challenging than it appears. On the surface, they may seem straightforward, but upon closer examination, they necessitate significant alterations to one's lifestyle, daily routine, and behavior. Streamlining these changes will undoubtedly pose difficulties, and anyone claiming otherwise is being dishonest. Nevertheless, it's essential to emphasize that the outcomes and the positivity they bring are worth the commitment.

Not everyone possesses the inner resolve to simply decide to transform their life. Resolutions serve as a glaring example of how many individuals talk a big game but fail to follow through with action. While I can't provide a foolproof strategy for adhering to your personal improvement plan, I can offer some helpful techniques.

Each of these methods is straightforward to implement, cost-free, and consumes minimal time. Select the ones that resonate with you, and experiment to devise a system that suits your unique needs.

1. **Progress Diaries:** Writing may not be everyone's preferred method, so if it doesn't appeal to you, there's no obligation to pursue it. However, maintaining some form of journal, log, or record of your endeavors can work wonders for your mental state. Firstly, it aids in clarifying and organizing your thoughts, which can be highly therapeutic. Narrating your thoughts or activities for later reflection also assists in evaluating your efforts, pinpointing issues, and enhancing efficiency in your endeavors. It additionally serves as a constant reminder of your motivation and objectives. Over time, you'll be able to witness your progress at a glance, even if your desired results have not yet materialized. This tangible evidence underscores your commitment, and sometimes, that's all the motivation you require.

2. **Bullet Journals and Creative Planners:** In a similar vein, this option caters to those who desire to maintain a progress diary but aren't inclined towards lengthy written entries. Bullet journals are designed to be efficient and effective planners. While they primarily function as checklists that yield results, there exists a thriving community of individuals who infuse creativity into their bullet journals. You can craft customizable spreads for a variety of purposes. For instance, you might create a compilation of motivational quotes, integrate a progress bar to track your achievements or utilize them for long-term planning or daily task management. Generally, planners facilitate organization and scheduling, ensuring you stay on course and eliminate excuses and procrastination. They are enjoyable to use and can provide a dose of endorphins.

3. **Positive Reinforcement and Rewards:** Sometimes, combating negativity requires a dose of positivity. Celebrate your victories, no matter how small, even if it feels forced or insincere at first. Over time, this practice will become habitual, replacing self-criticism with self-kindness. Think of Pavlov and his dogs, who associated a bell with food due to repeated exposure. Similarly, redirect negative thoughts by countering them with positive affirmations. Eventually, positivity may become an automatic response. If all else fails, motivate yourself with the promise of a treat or reward each time you reach a milestone or adhere to your plan.

4. **Set Clear Goals:** Remember that your ultimate aim is not to remain in the present but to transform yourself. However, human nature dictates that you'll occasionally forget your objective. That's why it's crucial to define precisely what you desire. Document it in a manner that suits you, whether through a vision board, a friendly wager, or a commitment to rewiring your mindset to conquer negativity, depression, anxiety, and insecurity. Regardless of the method, you need tangible evidence of your aspirations. This closely aligns with the concept of journaling but isn't limited to it. As long as you possess proof that your journey is purposeful, you'll be better equipped to rekindle your determination. Don't hesitate to refine your goals as you progress.

Responsibility: Share with someone. Share with everyone. Share with yourself. Nobody desires failure, so when you're aware that people are observing, your innate drive to succeed intensifies. There might be a couple of downsides to this approach, as it requires a certain level of confidence and can trigger some fear of judgment. That's why it's crucial to carefully select your audience. All you need is someone, or a group of people, who will hold you accountable for your commitments. This could be a workout partner, a family member, or even your online followers and friends. Quitting becomes effortless when you don't have to answer for it, so ensure that if you ever veer off course, you'll have to explain yourself to someone. The person you turn to may also offer constructive feedback. If that's what you're seeking, just ensure they are both honest and kind.

Guidance: There's no shame in seeking assistance, and there are experts willing to assist you on your journey. You can opt for a life coach or a personal trainer, or it might be a matter of finding a motivational podcast to tune into occasionally. Social media can be beneficial in this regard as well. Facebook's 'groups' feature is known for connecting you with like-minded individuals who can serve as both a support system and a mentor. Reddit is brimming with communities dedicated to inspiring and uplifting others (my personal favorite is Free Compliments). Whether you need a gentle push in the right direction or you're simply looking for advice, tips, and guidance, there is an abundance of free resources available. You just need to discover them and choose the ones that resonate with you.

Utilize Technology: Don't underestimate the capabilities of your smartphone. It comes equipped with alarms, reminders, calendars, and access to a plethora of apps that can assist you in organizing your life. Consider apps like Headspace, which is highly recommended for meditation beginners. You can download calorie-tracking apps or use your phone to follow exercise routines through streaming videos. Your phone can serve as your diary, schedule, or a means of reaching out to others for assistance or accountability, as mentioned earlier.

Push Yourself: If all else fails, motivate yourself into action. If you aspire to take up jogging, the only way to achieve that goal is by getting off your couch and hitting the pavement. This principle applies to waking up early, engaging in workouts, practicing meditation, or consuming less-than-delicious but healthful foods that open the doors to happiness. Willpower is an underestimated force. Yours might need some refinement, but once again, you have to utilize it to develop it further. Overcome obstacles (without harming yourself). Sometimes, that's all you can do.

Lesson Learned

Positivity and happiness are physiological reactions that can be influenced by your way of life. In contrast, negativity often results from detrimental behaviors. Opting to rectify this situation represents the most effective method to recalibrate and enhance your mental outlook. While it may present challenges, the endeavor will undoubtedly prove its value. If you aspire to self-improvement, prioritizing self-care is imperative. Bid farewell to your unfavorable and unhealthy routines and heed the counsel of experts who advocate for nourishing meals, adequate rest, physical activity, and personal time.

Shift your focus from your current situation to your aspirations as the initial step toward revitalizing both your health and mindset.

Overall, your text is well-structured and conveys a clear message about the importance of positivity, self-improvement, and self-care. I made a few minor improvements in fluency and readability. It's now error-free and retains the original structure of your sentences.

Chapter 2: Stop Being a Bully

Have you ever encountered the saying, "If everyone around you seems unpleasant, perhaps you're the one with the attitude problem"? This phrase can be interpreted in various ways, but I prefer to view it as a cautionary reminder that we sometimes neglect to monitor our own emotions and attitudes, leading to unnecessary frustration with our surroundings. If we fail to manage ourselves, we may become irritable and take out our frustrations on innocent people, much like the common occurrence of road rage. Often, minor annoyances are blown out of proportion, resulting in road violence and, tragically, numerous deaths. Although the person experiencing road rage is solely responsible for their actions, they often justify it by claiming that "others don't know how to drive." Does this sound fair to you in any way?

While road rage is an extreme example, humans tend to exhibit such behavior regularly. Wondering why? It's rooted in our mindsets. We are wired to desire that others perceive us as positively as we perceive ourselves, likely stemming from a strong need to protect our image. One essay refers to this phenomenon as the "epidemic of infallibility" (Krugman, 2017), suggesting that influential individuals, particularly those in the public eye, have lost touch with humility and exploit their status to manipulate the narrative, even when they are clearly at fault.

Although it's important not to overlook such behavior, part of me understands why celebrities and public figures are adamant about defending their positions. When they make mistakes or are caught in the wrong, the audience often reacts with anger, demanding accountability. To err is human, but what's often omitted is that our mistakes, no matter how small, can cost us our reputations, careers, relationships, opportunities, and even the support of loved ones. It's natural to fear shame, even for minor missteps. The problem arises when we deny our mistakes, refusing to admit our faults. Our initial reaction is to deflect blame or rationalize that external factors, beyond our control or judgment, led to the error (Krauss Whitbourne, 2017).

So, what does this have to do with you potentially being a bully? It circles back to the road rage analogy. If you constantly perceive everyone else as problematic, it's likely that you're the source of the problem. The same attitude you employ to avoid acknowledging your own mistakes might also be why you're overly critical of yourself. This mindset drives you to blame the world for your negativity rather than recognizing your responsibility to take care of yourself. We're often quick to shift blame onto others for our problems, allowing us to evade personal growth.

But let's shift our focus to a more positive perspective. Acknowledging your flaws is a display of strength. While it may sometimes be insincere and used for damage control (as frequently observed with public figures), the consensus is that admitting guilt is the most authentic and crucial step in offering apologies, rectifying wrongs, and ultimately achieving forgiveness.

This is where you come in. The path to reconciling with your own personality begins with admitting that sometimes it's not all sunshine and rainbows. However, a new challenge emerges: insecurity. Just as we tend to exaggerate our innocence, we are equally capable of magnifying our imperfections. This self-criticism turns us into our own bullies, leading us down a path of negativity and self-sabotage.

It's imperative that you stop being so hard on yourself. For the remainder of this chapter, I will guide you on how to learn to appreciate yourself. By doing so, you'll not only gain self-respect but also set yourself on the path toward cultivating a positive mindset.

Why We Hate Ourselves

Self-esteem is a rather mysterious concept. Although it's challenging to precisely define its purpose or the reason for its existence, some theories suggest that it acts as a catalyst for self-preservation (as referenced in "Why Self-Esteem is Important and Its Dimensions," 2015). Essentially, self-esteem boils down to how you perceive your own value. If your self-esteem is high, you're less likely to adopt harmful, degrading, or depreciating behaviors. Individuals with elevated self-esteem tend to take better care of themselves and generally possess more positive qualities.

However, a significant issue arises. Our self-esteem is heavily influenced by those in our social sphere. It's not merely a matter of deciding that we matter and deserve better. People's opinions of us have a profound impact on our self-image. An intriguing study sheds light on this matter. Researchers employed MRI scans to observe changes in neural signals linked to self-perception. Participants were asked to upload their profiles to a database and then watch the reactions of over 100 strangers, who would either give their profiles a "thumbs up" or "thumbs down," akin to social media feedback. Moreover, the strangers were divided into groups, leading participants to anticipate positive feedback from certain groups over others. Unbeknownst to the participants, these 'strangers' were, in reality, generated by an algorithm.

This study not only demonstrated that our confidence dwindles when we fail to garner approval from others but also revealed that our self-esteem plunges even further when we expect to be liked but are not (as referenced in "Self-esteem Mapped in the Human Brain," 2017). This seems to align with the earlier theory that our public image serves us, and thus we fiercely safeguard it, even when we are in the wrong. It appears as though there's no easy victory when it comes to our self-perception.

So, why do we struggle with self-esteem? Why do we tend to have such low self-esteem when it's intended to propel us forward positively? Delving deep into this question requires a thorough understanding of psychology, and the concise answer is that we lack certainty due to numerous variables. Naturally, someone who has endured a lifetime of criticism from others is unlikely to hold themselves in high esteem. In other cases, factors such as mental health disorders, trauma, or a general predisposition toward negativity play a role.

The reason why others' opinions have such a potent influence on our self-perception remains somewhat ambiguous. Nonetheless, the prevailing psychological theory suggests that it's intrinsic to human nature and directly contributes to our survival. Primitive humans functioned as herd animals, and survival depended on group strength during migrations, hunting, or battling the elements. The stronger the group, the higher the odds of survival. Individuals deemed weak or undesirable were left behind as they slowed down or burdened the group, seen as a waste of resources. If you weren't liked or accepted, you were essentially abandoned to fend for yourself. This same survival instinct persists today (citing Formica, 2014).

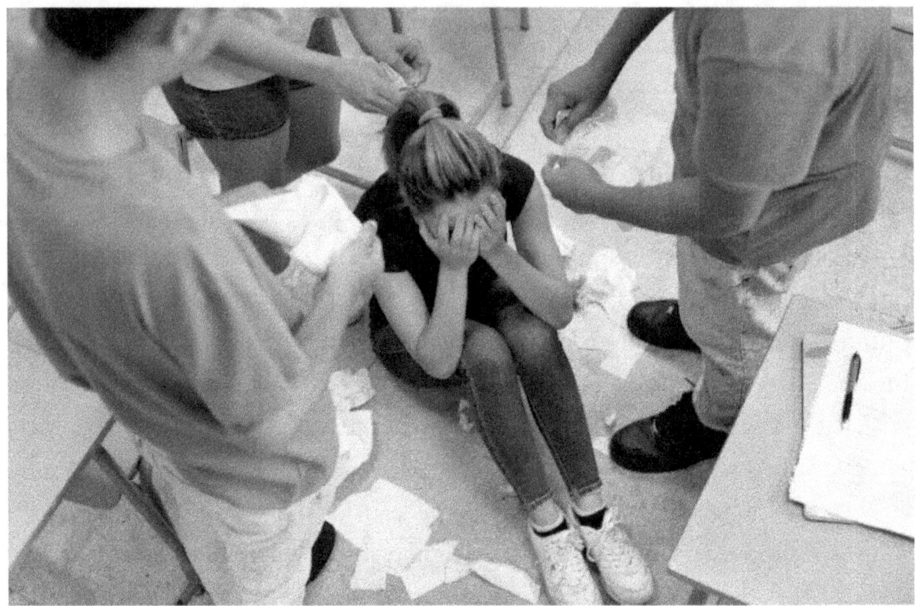

Expanding upon this theory, it is posited that we still feel threatened because, in modern times, humans have become their own primary predators. We are inherently social beings living in a world where failing to make a favorable impression can result in isolation. These instincts, aimed at proving our worth to avoid exclusion, provide the most plausible explanation for our fragile self-esteem.

However, it's essential to acknowledge that this perspective is fundamentally flawed. You are not a primitive human, and as long as you're a decent person, others' opinions should hold little significance. You won't be abandoned and devoured by prehistoric predators if people don't like you. I assure you of that. While it may be uncomfortable when people don't reciprocate our affections or validate our sense of self-worth, remember that it's "self"-worth, a determination that lies solely within you.

Hey there, you're awesome!

Or maybe even more awesome than you realize. I can assure you of this. Dealing with low self-esteem can be tough, but here's some fantastic news for those who feel like they're at the bottom of the ladder or don't quite fit into the bigger picture: you're deceiving yourself. Those pessimistic beliefs you've come to hold about yourself? They're baseless. And I can back this up with scientific evidence.

First, let me introduce you to a concept known as the "beautiful mess effect." This theory, supported by compelling evidence, dives into why the traits we dislike in ourselves are the very same ones we admire in others. In one particular experiment, participants were asked to imagine vulnerable situations, either involving themselves or others. One scenario included confessing romantic feelings to someone they were interested in. They were then asked to rate their own vulnerability or that of the person they were picturing in that situation. Almost every time, participants assessed their own vulnerability much more negatively than that of others (Source: "The 'Beautiful Mess' Effect: Other People View our Vulnerability More Positively than We Do," 2018). It's likely that this ties into our self-esteem and how it's influenced by external perceptions. We tend to see ourselves as especially weak in certain situations because we believe that's how others perceive us. However, the study proves the opposite. But there's another crucial aspect to consider.

This phenomenon is called the "spotlight effect," which means we tend to believe other people notice us more than they actually do. In the spotlight effect, the flaws you are so self-conscious about—whether it's a coffee stain on your shirt, the scent of your armpits, the size of your nose, or a nervous stutter—are magnified. But the truth is that these things are barely noticed by others. Following the beautiful mess effect, there's a good chance that even if they are noticed, observers don't think as negatively of you as you assume they do (Heflick, 2011).

You might think this is a fancy way of saying that you're less significant to those around you than you believe. However, that's not entirely accurate. It's simply a matter of something called egocentrism. Your life revolves around you because you are the lens through which you experience the world. You could call it self-centeredness, but in reality, everyone experiences life this way. You couldn't be anyone else even if you tried, and because you are the center of your own universe, your ego tends to exaggerate its role in the lives of others. This doesn't mean that you aren't important or unnoticed by others at all. What it does mean is that everyone is preoccupied with their own perceived flaws, whether it's a big nose, coffee stains, armpits, or stutters, to the point where they hardly judge yours.

Yes, we don't live in a utopian world, and there will always be people out there who may criticize your appearance, voice, or other aspects beyond your control. However, these individuals are generally unkind, and they constitute the minority, according to numerous psychological studies on this subject. Furthermore, do you know what we call individuals like that? Bullies. That's why it's crucial to stop being a bully to yourself.

In reality, you are far more impressive, attractive, or commendable than you give yourself credit for. Chances are, you are the only person casting yourself in a negative light (provided you are a decent, harmless individual who hasn't done anything wrong). Your insecurities are unfounded, and the only reason you magnify them in your mind is because you believe you aren't up to par with those around you.

It all boils down to fear. Fear of not being accepted, of being ridiculed, or of being abandoned to face imaginary threats. But those imaginary threats don't exist; they are figments of your imagination. Ultimately, the only person whose opinion truly matters is your own. If you start telling yourself that you are worthy, your ego might just begin to believe it. If you need a confidence boost, remember that even if you're a mess, other people will perceive you as a beautiful one.

So, now you must ask yourself why you are the only person you treat harshly. You wouldn't mock someone else for their appearance (or at least, I hope you wouldn't), and you wouldn't purposefully damage someone else's self-esteem. Hurting others isn't good for the soul because we are naturally empathetic, and we don't derive joy from others' suffering. Low self-esteem and negativity often go hand in hand, which is why we must put a stop to it. One way to achieve this is by treating yourself with the same compassion and kindness you extend to others. The first step in this process is nurturing your sense of self-confidence.

Confidence is Power

Consider this: confidence and self-esteem are not synonymous. Confidence, specifically self-confidence, reflects the trust you have in your own abilities. Self-esteem, on the other hand, pertains to your overall self-evaluation, independent of your abilities. It's essential to recognize that being confident doesn't always equate to having high self-esteem. This distinction is evident in celebrities who boldly perform in front of large audiences yet struggle with self-deprecating thoughts during interviews, battle eating disorders or body dysmorphia, or, in extreme cases, have such low self-regard that they resort to self-destructive behaviors like substance abuse or even suicide.

Building confidence doesn't guarantee an increase in self-esteem, but it's a crucial initial step that significantly facilitates the process of discovering and appreciating your worth. Moreover, fostering confidence tends to be more straightforward than nurturing self-esteem because confidence is self-sustaining and relies less on external opinions.

This link between confidence and achievement is pivotal because no one can strip away your accomplishments. When you feel proud, that sense of accomplishment is yours to keep. What's remarkable is that the actions you take to boost your confidence invariably contribute to enhancing your self-worth.

However, before delving into that aspect, it's worth highlighting the transformative potential of even a modest amount of confidence.

Consider individuals such as Oprah Winfrey, John Lennon, Angelina Jolie, and Marilyn Monroe, along with numerous others. They all grappled with self-esteem issues before they achieved fame (Ellis, 2019). Nevertheless, they possessed an unwavering belief in themselves, which propelled them to legendary status in their respective fields. Imagine if they had succumbed to their negative self-talk. Our world would be markedly different because their exceptional talents, which they recognized and diligently honed, have left an indelible mark on our lives. While Marilyn Monroe's story ended tragically, it's impossible to definitively attribute her fate to low self-esteem, mental health challenges, or a lapse in judgment. Regardless, like the others, she pursued her dreams with confidence and etched her name in history as one of the most iconic figures to have ever graced this Earth, all because she possessed the confidence to do so.

How about another illustration? In 1995, a young woman embarked on her journey as a writer. She crafted a synopsis of her creative concept and dispatched it to various publishers, accompanied by sample chapters. Astonishingly, she received rejection notices from 12 different publishing houses. The exact reasons behind these rejections remain a mystery, but it's plausible to assume there were diverse factors at play. Perhaps the publishers perceived shortcomings in her writing, or they harbored doubts about its marketability. Alternatively, it might have been a matter of personal taste or preference. The undeniable truth is that a dozen individuals, at various junctures in this young lady's life, delivered the verdict that she didn't meet their standards. However, she possessed an unwavering belief in her talent and refused to succumb to discouragement. Fast forward to 1997, and her book, "Harry Potter and the Philosopher's Stone," graced bookstore shelves. The woman in question, J.K. Rowling, who had weathered a dozen rejections, has indisputably become the preeminent author of our era. She achieved the remarkable distinction of being the first author to amass a billion-dollar fortune solely through writing. Her book series, the same one that had been turned away, went on to sell over 400 million copies worldwide, captivating the imaginations of people across the globe.

This narrative underscores the transformative power of self-belief and the importance of disregarding naysayers who dismiss your endeavors. It's a testament to the triumph of determination. But what if you find yourself lacking confidence? Well, here's a strategy to cultivate it.

Take Measures to Boost Self-Esteem: When you feel good about yourself, confidence naturally follows. Insecurities can arise from personal hygiene issues like body odor, uncomfortable or disheveled clothing, unkempt hair, or chipped nail polish. By taking pride in your appearance and maintaining personal hygiene, you eliminate the fear of being judged based on these factors. Moreover, you'll always be ready to seize unexpected opportunities without hesitation due to feeling unprepared. Reality dictates that people are inclined to scrutinize what they can see, as our primary sensory input comes from sight. While people may not notice you as much as you fear, they will undoubtedly take notice of conspicuous flaws. So, make an effort to improve your self-image by grooming and dressing well, even if there's no one around. I assure you that you'll appreciate yourself much more when your armpits don't smell like onions, and others will too.

Organize Your Surroundings: Building upon the previous point, your physical environment speaks volumes about you and invites judgments from others. If your workspace is chaotic, papers are in disarray, or last year's sandwich remnants have attracted rodents, people may form negative opinions about you. While the exterior isn't always an accurate reflection of the interior, it can significantly influence perceptions. Much like the importance of brushing your teeth, disposing of trash, making your bed, and maintaining an organized living space, these habits command respect from others and, more importantly, foster self-respect.

Explore New Endeavors: Confidence can be nurtured through the acquisition of skills and talents, as they provide concrete evidence of your abilities and may even instill a sense of pride that compels you to share your talents with the world. However, there's no immediate pressure to do so. For now, simply having something to be proud of suffices. If you already possess a skill or talent, invest more time and energy in honing it. Share it with others, even in unconventional places. Consider teaching it to someone else; the sense of importance and accomplishment that accompanies this can be profound. If you're struggling to identify a particular skill or talent, explore areas of interest and commit to learning something new.

Prepare Yourself for Success:

Embracing new interests or courses can seem overwhelming, but there's a simple strategy to ease into it. Start with tasks that are undemanding, ones you're sure to excel in. Everyone relishes victory, and witnessing your own accomplishments will significantly elevate your self-assurance. It could be something as lighthearted as dabbling in finger painting if that's what it takes. The key is to enjoy yourself and give it your all, no matter how trivial it may seem.

Avoid Your Triggers:

Occasionally, our circumstances can pull us down, so if you recognize the factors that make you feel downhearted, steer clear of them. Cease spending time with individuals who sap your positivity. Refrain from taking risky shortcuts in a haste to reach your destination. Stop fixating on others' art, creations, or appearances if it only leads to self-comparison and a sense of inadequacy. If you can't evade your triggers, make a concerted effort to manage or conquer them.

Catalog Your Achievements:

Much like keeping a progress journal to sustain motivation, acknowledging your own accomplishments can ignite your confidence. Declare your strengths. Compile a list that you can revisit when your self-esteem wanes and you need a reminder of your capabilities. The objective is to emphasize your strong points, not your weaknesses.

Show Kindness:

Validation from others often bolsters our self-esteem, so extend kindness to others. It may sound somewhat superficial and insincere to perform good deeds solely for personal gain, but the recipient need not be aware of your motivation. They will feel uplifted because you've assisted them, and you will experience a sense of fulfillment. So, where's the harm? While confidence primarily stems from within, occasionally hearing praise from others is precisely what it takes to reinforce that belief. This principle of kindness applies to yourself as well. Speak kindly to yourself. It may sound clichéd, but it's effective.

Prioritize Self-Care:

You should already be prioritizing this (haven't you learned anything from the first chapter?). When you succeed in your personal objectives, your confidence will naturally soar, especially if it involves challenging feats that many others struggle with. Quit smoking. Manage your diet. Hit the gym. It will enhance your appearance, boost your well-being, and ultimately align with my initial point of taking the necessary steps to enhance your self-esteem.

Fake it Until You Become it:

Do these steps feel too arduous? Skip them all and simply feign confidence. I assure you that no one will detect the difference, not even yourself.

How to Like Yourself

At some point in your life, you will inevitably experience a period of diminished confidence or even a complete self-esteem crisis. So, what should you do when this happens, and how can you nourish your self-esteem to prevent these dips in self-perception? I'll be honest; you might not like what I'm about to suggest.

The only effective path to repairing your damaged self-esteem is through therapy (if it's necessary due to a psychological disorder) or personal transformation. These steps won't come easy, but they are essential. If you don't make a sincere effort to implement these changes, you'll likely never become a positive person. However, if you do commit to this process, bearing in mind that it won't magically fix everything overnight, you will gradually become your own ally. Those hurtful inner voices resembling a bully will start to fade over time. Eventually, those instincts to be harsh on yourself will diminish, and your mindset will shift towards one of confidence, self-worth, and positivity.

Recognize Your Flaws! Let's go back to the beginning of this chapter, where I mentioned our reluctance to admit when we're wrong. Frankly, that kind of behavior is unappealing, and nobody likes someone who behaves that way. You don't need to rush around apologizing to every person you've ever wronged, lied to, or offended. Still, you must have an honest conversation with yourself. Be authentic. You'll discover that you actually like yourself more when you stop pretending to be something you're not – perfect. No one is perfect. The sooner you release the pressure to be flawless, the more relaxed, likable, and positive you'll become.

Highlight Your Strengths! Once again, focus on your strengths. If you're insecure about your teeth, for instance, find aspects of your appearance that you genuinely appreciate. Perhaps you have fantastic hair; embrace it by wearing a stylish headband or trying a new hair color. Experiment with a different style or flaunt it as much as you can. By emphasizing what you like about yourself, you'll divert attention away from your insecurities, leading to reduced anxiety, and that spotlight we talked about will dim. Apply this principle to all aspects of your life, from your talents and personality to your job. Maybe you're not great at public speaking, but you excel at writing. Concentrate on that. If singing isn't your forte, but you enjoy dancing, ditch the karaoke bars and head to a dance class or nightclub. Instead of zooming in on your self-criticism, redirect that energy to showcase your strengths.

Learn to Enjoy Solitude! Strangely enough, we often dislike ourselves the most when we're alone. Look at the majority of single people in the world – loneliness, a genuine problem, can lead to feelings of unworthiness. If someone you're interested in rejects you, you might turn inward and question what's wrong with you, rather than accepting that they simply don't share your feelings. It's crucial to learn to be content in your own company. To achieve this, you'll need to fill the voids left by others. If you're single and feeling down because you lack a partner for romantic evenings, take yourself out on a date. Go all out – dress up, dine at an upscale restaurant, splurge on theater tickets, or beat your own high score at the arcade. What's holding you back? Exactly, nothing.

Or, if you're a bit hesitant (which is perfectly fine), start with small steps like enjoying solo movie nights, preparing a delightful meal for yourself, or indulging in activities you love in moments of solitude. You'll discover that you're pretty amazing when you're not tearing yourself down.

Say "Screw It!" Here's a fun idea: stop caring and give your worst for the sheer thrill of it. If you're uncomfortable without makeup, I challenge you to go makeup-free. If you avoid swimming because of a noticeable scar, put on the skimpiest swimsuit you can find and wear that scar as a badge of honor. If anyone has the audacity to comment, look them straight in the eyes and confidently utter these words: "So what?" You can even replace it with cheeky phrases like "Yes, and?", "Problem?", or the snarkiest of all, "I know!"

You won't believe how empowering this can be. Many of our insecurities stem from the fear that others will notice and exploit our flaws. But if you're the one who acknowledges them, you take away the power from those who might be mean-spirited enough to use them against you. It's quite amusing to watch people attempt to judge you and then struggle to justify themselves. It's not only satisfying but also a guaranteed way to savor a taste of your own awesomeness.

Embrace Your Past without Regret! Understand that altering the past is beyond your grasp. The errors you've committed can't be reversed, so it's wise to grant yourself forgiveness. If you continually yearn for your past glory days, when youth and freedom prevailed, and you appeared a million times cooler than your current self, you'll only plunge into melancholy. If you persistently berate yourself for past decisions that don't align with your desires, you'll foster resentment towards yourself. What's done is done. Reflect on it, remember it, but don't dwell in regret. You still possess time. Revel in your present self, not the person you once were or the one you aspire to become.

Cease the Habit of Comparing Yourself to Others! This habit will naturally subside when you master acknowledging your own imperfections and recognize that perfection is unattainable. Here's the reality check: You are unaware of what resides in the hearts of others. Even the most accomplished, attractive, and esteemed individuals you encounter may carry bitterness, misery, or emptiness within. You lack insight into their hidden struggles, so there's no valid reason to believe you fall short in comparison. Perhaps they secretly envy your life. Perhaps their existence is so challenging that they wouldn't wish it upon anyone, not even their worst foes. You'll never truly know because some burdens remain concealed.

Social media has desensitized us to the ordinary. We craft a facade of glamour and composure, but in truth, most of us grapple with imperfections. If you must draw inspiration from others, do so with the awareness that you're ignorant of their personal narratives. We all wrestle with our undisclosed battles. Be appreciative of your current circumstances. You never know who may be enduring far greater hardships than you.

Refrain from Magnifying Your Imperfections! Lastly, it's essential to implement the insights from this entire chapter and realize that the spotlight effect has inflated your ego. Your insecurities likely aren't as severe as you perceive them to be. Unless you find yourself in dire straits or deeply in love, the opinions of others hold little significance. Ground yourself and acknowledge that you are your harshest critic. The only remaining step is to cease the nitpicking and self-criticism. Being kind to yourself is the way forward, and it's far more admirable than being excessively critical.

Lesson Learned

Self-esteem plays a pivotal role in fostering a positive outlook on life, yet it predominantly hinges on external evaluations from others. Paradoxically, our egos tend to make us self-absorbed, often causing us to assume that people are scrutinizing us when, in reality, they may not even be thinking about us. Confidence, on the other hand, reflects our trust in our own capabilities. Although it differs from self-esteem, these two concepts are frequently interchanged and tend to intertwine. If you aspire to cultivate a more optimistic disposition, it becomes essential to enhance both your self-esteem and confidence.

To combat negative self-talk, bolster your confidence, elevate your self-esteem, and nurture a brighter mindset, it becomes imperative to establish a genuine friendship with yourself and extend the same kindness towards yourself that you readily offer to others."

Chapter 3: Declutter Your Life

The primary focus lies in the initial two steps: addressing your well-being and reshaping your self-perception, as they hold utmost significance. This is why I dedicated substantial time to elucidate them. I strongly advise revisiting these steps as necessary and placing great importance on mastering them, as they yield the most profound impact on your perspective. If you embark on your journey towards positivity with this mindset, I assure you that navigating the subsequent five steps will become considerably more manageable.

Nevertheless, recognizing the intensity of the initial two steps, let's momentarily shift our attention away from the weighty aspects and delve into a simpler yet highly effective endeavor: decluttering. While it may sound like a mundane task, trust me, it stands as one of the most therapeutic approaches to banishing negative thoughts.

Our surroundings have a profound impact on us, and when we encircle ourselves with negativity, it inevitably molds our outlook. It's time to physically eliminate the elements that dampen your spirits.

A Look at Minimalism

You've likely encountered this lifestyle concept previously, but I wouldn't be surprised if you dismissed it without delving deeper. There's a considerable amount of confusion surrounding it. Minimalism doesn't equate to a frugal existence or living with the bare essentials. It isn't a political statement or a fleeting fashion trend. Instead, minimalism signifies a commitment to maintaining only what you genuinely value and need, with the aim of simplifying your life, nurturing your mental well-being, and attaining inner tranquility.

There exist five distinct forms of minimalism, and although you aren't obliged to wholeheartedly adopt any particular one, I suggest selecting the one that resonates most with you and employing its ideals as the foundation for your decluttering journey. It's essential to emphasize here that you need not fully embrace minimalism to become a more positive individual. However, the reasoning behind it is sound, and there's no harm in experimenting with it just for the sake of curiosity. You may discover that it suits you well.

1. **Essentialism:** Often viewed as the most stringent form of minimalism, essentialism centers on retaining and utilizing only what is unquestionably essential. In this approach, sentimentality, extravagance, and waste are discouraged. If you don't require more than one loaf of bread, refrain from purchasing excess. Those old postcards you've clung to, even though it's now 2020 and snail mail is nearly extinct? It's time to bid them farewell. You adhere solely to what contributes to your survival, comfort, and happiness.

2. **Enough ism:** The name itself conveys the essence of this minimalistic philosophy. You retain what you perceive as "enough" and dispense with the surplus. In the aforementioned example, perhaps you might find a use for a postcard at some point, but just one will suffice. Amassing a stack of them is deemed excessive and thus superfluous. If you live alone, a single set of dishes is adequate; there's no need for an entire cupboard full. With this decluttering approach, you still have the pleasure of

keeping items you cherish, as long as they aren't deemed wasteful or redundant.

3. **Eco-Minimalism:** This variant has been gaining traction, primarily due to the looming environmental crisis. Unlike the previous two, the central objective of eco-minimalism is to minimize your ecological footprint to the best of your ability. This may entail entirely eliminating meat from your diet or substantially reducing meat consumption. Plastic usage is discouraged, while recycling is actively encouraged. Eco-minimalists also strive to conserve energy and contribute to reducing the Earth's waste issue as infrequently as possible.

4. **Experientialism:** Among the five, this is my personal favorite. Experientialism advocates a heightened awareness of how your possessions truly affect your well-being. Adherents of this philosophy strive to be non-materialistic and actively prioritize experiences over material possessions. Budget travelers and backpackers inherently embody the principles of experientialism, even if they don't explicitly identify as such. Sentiment is permitted, but only if it serves a meaningful purpose.

5. **Soul Minimalism:** Best suited for those seeking a shift in their mindset, soul minimalism shares similarities with experientialism but places greater emphasis on the impact you impart on the world rather than what the world imparts on you. Soul minimalists practice mindfulness and endeavor to reduce negativity in their surroundings. In this context, sentimentality isn't frowned upon, but detachment is crucial, akin to the principles of Buddhist philosophy.

In all these variations, the core tenet of minimalism remains consistent: if an item holds no significance and serves no purpose, it's best to release it. Excess is viewed negatively because it embodies wastefulness, and the primary focus should be on maximizing your time on Earth, rather than accumulating possessions. In simple terms, minimalism is a liberating lifestyle that affords you more time and space for a fulfilling and positive existence.

Take the Trash Out

Which path resonated with you the most? If you're still uncertain, I strongly suggest embracing the experientialist approach, although soul minimalism is also a great option. What I urge you to do is assess your living or working environment and eliminate anything that doesn't contribute to your comfort, survival, or joy.

This recommendation is supported by scientific evidence. Clutter can lead to feelings of anxiety, stress, and even depression because it overwhelms our senses, pushing them into overdrive and fostering negative thoughts and emotions (Carter, 2012). Moreover, clutter can harbor dirt and have adverse effects on your health. It can pose risks, such as in the case of a fire, and can erode your self-esteem due to concerns about judgment or inadequacy.

Residing or working in a clean and stress-free space can significantly enhance your mood and mindset. You'll experience greater comfort, a heightened sense of safety, improved self-esteem, and enhanced productivity and creativity. If you choose to follow the minimalist path, you'll create more physical and metaphorical room for the things that truly matter to you and deserve your focus.

So, give it a shot, and always remember: if it lacks meaning and necessity, it's time to bid it farewell. You'll be astonished at the profound positive impact this will have on your mental well-being.

Birds of a Feather

Decluttering extends beyond just organizing your physical belongings. It encompasses every aspect of your life. What better way to rid yourself of negativity than by distancing yourself from individuals who consistently bring you down?

To be clear, I'm not suggesting you harm anyone, though I understand why you might be tempted to do so at times. Instead, I propose decluttering your social circle. Apply the same principle you use to keep your physical space free of unnecessary clutter and cut ties with those who don't hold significant meaning in your life. If ending friendships seems too daunting, consider creating some distance.

As humans, we are inherently social creatures. So much so that we often assume others dislike us, leading to a devaluation of our self-worth. Now that you understand how and why people impact you, it's crucial to contemplate removing genuinely toxic individuals from your life.

I acknowledge that this can be challenging, especially when you care about these individuals. However, your negative feelings may result from their manipulation, cruelty, meanness, or outright abuse. Identify what you should no longer tolerate and take steps to eliminate it from your life. Of course, do this when you're ready, but the sooner you embark on this journey, the quicker you'll create space for positivity and positive influences.

As the saying goes, "Birds of a feather flock together." Make more time for those who uplift you and contribute positively to your life, and less for those who drag you down.

By the way, this principle extends to social media as well. That person you find yourself arguing with on Facebook? Remove them. That Twitter feed that constantly irritates you but you can't stop scrolling through? Unfollow it. Those YouTube channels and Instagram accounts that consistently frustrate you, as well as any contacts that disrupt your peace – declutter them all. You owe no explanations, and there's no need for guilt. It's for your own well-being.

Soul Food

After decluttering your online feeds, you'll notice that the time you spend on your favorite apps, services, or websites becomes more enjoyable. Instead of easily getting frustrated, you'll often find amusement in the content you come across, leading to a heightened sense of relaxation. This transformation occurs because our emotional state is significantly influenced by what we expose ourselves to. Neglecting to tidy up our preferred platforms exposes us to vast amounts of undesirable content, such as endless arguments that drain our energy or more distressing material like violent news and stories of prejudice and corruption. Even the television shows and music we consume can contribute to our discomfort. It's crucial to pay attention to how these things affect your emotions. If they have a negative impact, you'll know what steps to take.

Furthermore, advertising constantly urges us to consume without restraint. Coupled with the seemingly idyllic lives of those we see around us, it's no wonder we may start feeling inferior. However, this is a deceptive perception.

Your wavering self-esteem bears the responsibility, even in the realm of the internet and interactions with people you don't personally know.

The good news is that you can fine-tune and optimize your social media experiences. Conceal the posts that don't resonate with you, and each platform will adapt to show you less similar content. Block pages and accounts that don't align with your interests, while actively supporting those that do. Your feeds will then be tailored to your preferences, resulting in a much happier online experience.

Lesson Learned

Minimalism offers an efficient means of simplification, and this simplification can greatly benefit your mental well-being and perspective. While it can be challenging to part with certain belongings or individuals, our surroundings play a significant role in shaping us, and our environment can influence our emotions. Accumulated clutter often triggers a cascade of negative feelings, while maintaining relationships with toxic individuals unquestionably damages one's self-esteem. Embracing minimalism is a gradual and ongoing process, much like any other commitment, but it is advisable to incorporate it into your life, even in small ways, to enhance your overall perspective. The essential aspect involves discerning what truly serves your well-being and letting go of what does not.

Chapter 4: Change

Is decluttering a fashionable notion, isn't it? Well, the time for leisure and amusement has ended, and now we must confront the stark realities behind the gloominess of your outlook and mindset. Negativity breeds negativity, and sometimes, it truly is that straightforward. Recall Chapter Two, where we delved deeply into the examination of how inflated our self-perceptions tend to be. We, as egocentric beings, often overestimate our importance to such an extent that we'll rationalize our known imperfections and blunders just to preserve our image.

But who are you deceiving? If you genuinely desire a more positive mindset, you must acknowledge that at times, you might be the source of toxicity. Your conduct could be your own worst adversary. If you persist in repeating negative behaviors and then dismiss them due to the widespread belief in one's infallibility, you will gradually slip into a deceptive sense of self-worth and invincibility that will ultimately prove detrimental in the long haul.

One potential consequence of this is that you may blind yourself to your own falsehoods, while others suffer the consequences. They may distance themselves or confront you, and you—insisting that you've done nothing wrong—will convince yourself that the world is conspiring against you. You'll harbor resentment toward the world, and question why no one likes you, and those negative whispers you're striving so hard to banish will resurface.

It is imperative to be honest with yourself. If you are contributing negativity to the world, how can you hope to cultivate the opposite? Regardless of one's beliefs about karma, we can all agree that we should treat others as we wish to be treated. Yet, on occasion, you treat people poorly. It's high time you cleaned up your act.

Taking the Reins

The term 'toxic' is frequently used casually nowadays to describe almost anything mildly unpleasant. However, toxic behavior carries much greater gravity. According to psychologist Nancy Irwin in a report (Langslet, 2018), a toxic individual is someone who displays emotional instability, engages in abusive actions, and offers no support. There exists a significant distinction between someone who is simply bothersome and someone who is genuinely toxic. It's possible to fall into both categories, which is why it's crucial to identify your own warning signs; otherwise, your negative conduct will persist and weigh you down.

You may not exhibit toxicity to the extent of manipulating, invalidating, or causing harm to others, but you might be directing toxicity inward, harming yourself. Even if your negativity isn't as extreme, nobody is entirely blameless, and they cannot absolve themselves of all responsibility. Your negativity or toxicity might be a response to something, but it remains negative and toxic, thus posing a problem.

In general, humans tend to operate on autopilot, following their feelings and instincts without truly reflecting on their actions. This leads us to overlook many of our own mistakes.

A critical step toward improving your attitude involves taking control of your behavior and consciously choosing to be kinder, more positive, and more considerate of both yourself and those around you. No one else can do this for you. However, it's wise to seek input from those who know you well to identify areas where your attitude requires adjustment. If you decide to take this path, be open to listening to their perspective. This is not the time to defend yourself or assert infallibility. Instead, it's an opportunity to view yourself through the eyes of others in order to make positive changes.

Seeing Red

Toxic characteristics can manifest in various ways, but broadly speaking, an individual is considered toxic when they display manipulative, destructive, abusive (in any form, whether physical, psychological, sexual, verbal, or emotional), and narcissistic behavior.

The following are indicators that identify a toxic individual. It's essential to distance yourself from people who exhibit such conduct in your life or inner circle, but it's equally important to take responsibility for the traits you exhibit.

1. **Neglect after initial interest:** Toxic individuals tend to focus on others until their desires are fulfilled and then lose interest. Their emphasis lies in the pursuit rather than the relationship itself. While it's not necessary to provide constant attention to everyone, if someone consistently disregards your needs when you should be a priority, it's considered toxic. Reflect on how you treat those who matter to you; you might inadvertently be neglecting others.

2. **Devaluing others:** Constantly undermining, belittling, or disparaging others is clearly wrong and a significant warning sign to avoid such individuals. Consider how you communicate with people. Do you dwell on their imperfections and vulnerabilities? Do you offer compliments as readily as criticisms? If not, it's crucial to reflect and work on this behavior.

3. **Dishonesty:** While minor fibs are generally tolerated, habitual dishonesty, especially about oneself, erodes trust. Dishonesty and distrust often go hand in hand. The inability to trust someone can lead to other negative consequences, such as paranoia or, in extreme cases, obsession and control.

4. **Unresponsiveness:** Not every emotionally distant person is toxic; some may be battling depression. Determining the difference requires careful attention. Toxic individuals, however, consistently display a lack of regard for others and their concerns. Ask yourself if you genuinely care

or respond when someone shares something with you, and whether you possess empathy for others.

5. **Ignorance:** Ignorance alone is not always a sign of toxicity; some individuals genuinely lack understanding. The issue arises when this ignorance becomes egocentric. Toxic individuals are oblivious to their own flaws, unable to acknowledge or even perceive them. Consequently, they cannot comprehend how their negative actions or mistakes impact others.

6. **Gaslighting** is closely related to ignorance. It entails a form of psychological manipulation where the offender convinces the victim that they are mistaken when confronted about their negativity. Even when presented with evidence of their wrongdoing, gaslighters will find ways to rationalize their belief that the victim is to blame.

7. **Narcissism,** a term often used indiscriminately, differs significantly from vanity. Vanity refers to a simple self-appreciation displayed arrogantly. On the other hand, narcissism, when it becomes toxic, involves believing that you are superior, better, and more important than those around you. It centers on prioritizing your own needs, consistently making everything about you. This toxic trait is typically accompanied by a lack of empathy and an insatiable need for attention and admiration.

8. **Control** is another characteristic of toxic individuals. They tend to exert control over the people in their circle, whether it's by dictating what they should wear or denying them privileges that they should inherently have as free-thinking adults. Detecting control can be challenging since different relationships have varying dynamics. However, if you notice yourself making decisions for others, even without an invitation, it may be invasive behavior, indicating that you could be a toxic presence.

9. These characteristics don't always manifest simultaneously in toxic individuals. They can either be dominant traits or appear sporadically, possibly directed toward specific people only. A person may exhibit only a few of these traits, but that doesn't negate their status as a negative, toxic individual. Now, it's crucial to introspect and determine if you might be that person.

Mindfulness

Mindfulness constitutes a form of meditation, as previously discussed in Chapter One as a reminder, emphasizing that it's not an optional practice; it requires dedication to eventually achieve proficiency. At its core, mindfulness involves the skill of directing your attention, not in a haphazard manner, but with a precise focus on the immediate present. Its primary objective is simply to recognize and embrace your current experiences without the urge to dissect, criticize, or alter them. Because it belongs to the realm of meditation, it serves therapeutic purposes, promoting relaxation, mental clarity, and even physical well-being. Encouraging research indicates that mindfulness holds the potential to reduce blood pressure, alleviate pain, and improve both sleep quality and cardiovascular health (Advantages of Mindfulness, 2019).

Numerous proponents of minimalism also incorporate mindfulness into their decluttering efforts. By thoroughly observing your surroundings, you become more decisive in determining whether to retain or discard items. Furthermore, mindfulness aids in nurturing healthier relationships by enhancing attentiveness during interactions and experiences, fostering greater consideration for others' emotions.

Crucially, mindfulness empowers you to introspect. By attentively monitoring your actions, words, sensations, thoughts, and reactions, you gain insights into which choices may be detrimental and how they impact those around you. Additionally, mindfulness serves as a tool to combat self-criticism. It amplifies the intensity of your negative and intrusive thoughts and emotions, highlighting the harshness with which you often treat yourself. Mindfulness inspires a shift towards kindness, consideration, and positivity.

Mindfulness instills a habit of thinking before acting, deciding, or following through, reinforcing the importance of aligning actions with words. The key lesson in mindfulness is that once you act, there's no reversing your choices, and if negativity arises, it cannot be retracted. Mindfulness compels you to confront your true self instead of operating on autopilot. Many individuals may find this self-reflection uncomfortable, yet it often serves as the catalyst for positive change.

Once you confront your inner shadows, continued mindfulness practice tends to guide you back toward the light. It emerges as a highly recommended approach for cultivating positivity since, despite the stark revelation of your imperfections, it unveils the beauty within you. Mindfulness equips us to savor life to the fullest and relish every moment.

Pay close attention. Mindfulness can take various forms and serve different purposes, but the easiest way to incorporate it into your life is by making a deliberate effort to be fully aware of your surroundings and experiences. Start with something small, such as savoring a cup of coffee or immersing yourself in a song. Engage all your senses while you partake in these activities. What does your coffee's aroma remind you of? How does it feel against your lips? What sounds accompany each sip? As you swallow, does it offer a comforting warmth? Reflect on your emotional state during this coffee break. Are you genuinely enjoying it, or is it merely a necessity to keep you awake? These are just a few examples of the things we often leave on autopilot.

The same applies to music. Select a favorite song and truly listen to it. You'll uncover nuances you've overlooked, like the faint cymbal tinkling or the vocalist's subtle breaths between words. You might even detect imperfections, like a missed beat or an editing mistake. Take a moment to observe yourself as well. Are your fingers tapping absentmindedly? Are you feeling restless? Does the music stir a desire to dance, shout, or cry? Consider why it's your favorite song and which lyric resonates with your inner emotions.

You get the idea. Utilize this same technique to practice mindfulness in all aspects of your life, from your conversations to your inner thoughts, from your insecurities to your self-appreciation. The deeper your immersion in these experiences, the better you'll comprehend them. This understanding will enable you to work on changing what you dislike and highlighting what truly matters.

Words as Weapons

Recall your childhood when you were taught the saying that "sticks and stones may break your bones, but words will never cause harm"? Let's collectively share a laugh over how untrue that statement can be. Often, words inflict deeper wounds than physical blows, as they have a way of cutting to the core. If someone were to physically assault you right now, it would undoubtedly hurt a great deal. However, with time, physical wounds heal, and the pain subsides. Unfortunately, the same cannot always be said for the hurtful words people have spoken to you, even if they were uttered years ago.

This concept is closely connected to our self-esteem. We all seek the approval of others, so when they offer criticism and disapproval, it can be soul-crushing, quite literally.

I recall a woman I know who has long been insecure about her chin. This insecurity began in grade school when a boy teased her, comparing her chin to that of Johnny Bravo's. Today, in her thirties, that emotional wound has never truly healed. She told me that she hadn't even noticed her chin's oblong shape until that boy pointed it out. Words possess a power that often goes underestimated, and if there's any technique in this book akin to ancient magic, it's harnessing the power of words to your advantage.

I've previously mentioned my lack of enthusiasm for mantras, and I'm sure many share that sentiment. When you're grappling with maintaining a positive mindset, it's unlikely that you'll find motivation in mindlessly repeating empty phrases throughout the day. Mantras tend to be the furthest thing from your mind, and unless you genuinely believe in every word you utter, they won't be of much assistance.

However, assertions are a different story. The beauty of assertions lies in their simplicity and practicality. You don't need to allocate any additional time or effort to use them, apart from being mindful of your words, which should come naturally with practice.

Once, I listened to a motivational speaker who introduced me to the concept of the "power of yet," which significantly altered my perspective on the world and myself. It became apparent just how unkind I had been to myself. The power of yet is a straightforward idea. Rather than manifesting negatives through your words, you transform them into positives by adding one tiny word: "yet." So, instead of stating, "I'm not happy," try saying, "I'm not happy yet." This implies that you acknowledge the current negativity but refuse to succumb to it. It conveys a sense of hope, indicating your belief in the possibility of a positive change. Apply this principle to something simpler: "I don't have a job" describes an unemployed individual, whereas "I don't have a job yet" portrays a job seeker. Do you see the difference?

There is absolutely no valid reason to demean yourself, yet many of us engage in self-deprecation daily without realizing it. The next time you catch yourself in a self-deprecating moment, take note and then transform self-deprecation into self-appreciation. This will prove to be more effective than any mantra ever could be because assertions are not just words; they are beliefs.

Lesson Learned

At times, you can be the source of the issue. It's quite common to fall into the trap of self-victimization when you fail to recognize your own warning signs. However, when you refuse to acknowledge that you're not always a stellar individual, it can impede your personal development and your quest for a positive mindset. Engaging in mindfulness can help you become aware of your own errors and foster greater self-appreciation. Through mindfulness, you'll develop kindness towards everyone, including yourself, and become more cautious about your words and actions. Once you've acknowledged your own negativity, you can actively strive to transform it into something positive. Assertions carry more weight than mantras or self-deception and possess an underestimated influence that can shift your perspective with minimal effort on your part.

Chapter 5: Sh*t Happens (Deal with It!)

You might resent me for this; I have a strong sense of it. Before I unveil the startling revelation behind your potential resentment, I'd like to pose a question: What drives your desire to combat your negative thoughts? There are apparent reasons, such as a longing for greater happiness or the determination to accomplish something meaningful in your life. However, I can't help but ponder whether you might be somewhat misguided.

I've invested numerous pages in instilling positivity into your psyche. I've put you through a mental boot camp, emphasizing that to become a positive person, you must confront the fact that much of your negativity is self-imposed. And here's the reason I'll empathize if you decide not to remain my friend:

On occasion, your efforts will prove futile, rendering everything I've conveyed thus far inconsequential. Why, you ask? Because perpetual happiness is an unattainable ideal. Sometimes, there is no silver lining. Occasionally, the grass isn't greener on the other side; it's parched and weathered, adorned with unsavory elements that attract flies and ants. Occasionally, you'll find yourself profoundly unhappy and overwhelmingly negative, and there won't be a remedy.

Sustained happiness isn't just unnatural; it can also be detrimental. According to a report by Hosie (2017), unceasing positivity can hinder your emotional growth. The report goes on to assert that while positivity is undoubtedly a desirable emotion, it isn't always fitting and doesn't consistently serve our best interests.

Let's consider a catastrophic scenario—a truly dreadful event, such as a natural disaster or a terrorist attack. Now, envision the individuals affected by it dancing joyfully in the street as it unfolds, offering praise to the heavens for this splendid, jubilant day.

That would be an aberrant reaction. When you contemplate the genuine definition of negativity, it becomes evident. Oxford defines the term as "the expression of criticism of, or pessimism about, something." At times, negativity is indispensable. It's how dissatisfaction, pain, or despondency materialize within us, and at times, it can be a lifesaver. Negative feelings about someone or something often prompt us to avoid potential dangers. If you don't enjoy something or feel uncomfortable in a situation, your negativity can serve as a signal to pause and remove yourself from the predicament.

Negativity is what enables us to detect warning signs in others, sense impending danger, or assert ourselves when necessary. In and of itself, it isn't inherently negative; it only becomes problematic when taken to extremes. So, when is it acceptable to embrace negativity, aside from situations involving terror or safety concerns? More importantly, when should you manage your negativity rather than combat it head-on?

Only Human

The reality is that it's more beneficial to acquire effective skills for processing your negative emotions, enabling you to address them and maintain your psychological and emotional well-being. Denying the existence of negativity isn't conducive to your overall health. This approach essentially involves suppressing your emotions, which can lead to mental and physical ailments, primarily due to the accumulation of unnoticed anxiety (Hendel, 2018).

Humans do not experience emotions in isolation. Consider Christmas Eve, for instance, when you eagerly anticipate opening your presents the next day. You're undoubtedly happy, but you also feel excitement, curiosity, wonder, charm, and perhaps even a touch of nervousness, wondering if your gifts will be appreciated by your friends and family.

Negativity operates similarly. Rarely, if ever, does one experience pure negativity. It's usually a mix of various dark emotions such as sadness, frustration, anger, guilt or shame, self-loathing, concern, and distrust, among others. By pretending to be fine, you're neglecting these stressful emotions, and they will accumulate within you until they find a way to surface. When we suppress our emotions, they tend to erupt unexpectedly, leading to arguments, hurtful comments, uncontrollable crying, or even destructive outbursts. Essentially, the more negativity you ignore, the more negative you become.

As a human being, you are entitled to moments of sadness, pain, anger, and occasional disillusionment with the world. What truly matters is not allowing negativity to dominate your life.

Experiencing a degree of distress that corresponds to your circumstances is normal. However, if you find yourself consistently overwhelmed by anguish for no apparent reason, it may be a sign of an underlying medical issue like a psychological disorder or hormonal imbalance. It's crucial to exercise discernment and mindfulness to determine whether your negativity is within the realm of normalcy.

For instance, if you've been enduring a prolonged period of adversity, it's understandable if you haven't been your usual self during that time. Sometimes, circumstances are beyond our control, and all we can do is endure the challenges. Yet, if everything around you is seemingly perfect, with no substantial complaints, and you still experience persistent dissatisfaction, emptiness, unexplained sadness, nervousness, or resentment, it's advisable to investigate potential underlying problems.

I'm not attempting to instill fear. Our moods naturally ebb and flow more than we often realize. However, it becomes concerning and detrimental to your well-being if you've been stuck in a prolonged emotional rut without a discernible cause.

In such instances, try not to be overly critical of yourself. Recall that nobody is flawless, and there is no shame in not feeling okay.

Self-Inflicted Suffering

While negativity is an inevitable part of life, suffering doesn't have to be. Often, we underestimate our ability to regulate our emotions and actions, especially when things aren't going well. Struggling, in its simplest form, means facing difficulties such as trying to keep up with someone or lifting a heavy object. On the other hand, suffering is a state of being that describes how you feel when something unfavorable occurs in your life, such as the loss of a loved one or the consequences of poorly thought-out decisions.

Frequently, we find ourselves suffering because we unintentionally prolong our own pain by not addressing it when it first arises. For instance, how often do you wait until you're in excruciating pain before seeing a doctor or dentist? After a breakup, do you allow your emotions to fester instead of working through them? How often do you sacrifice your own comfort and well-being to avoid confronting someone or speaking up about an issue?

Negativity is a natural part of the human experience, something we all grapple with at times. However, subjecting ourselves to prolonged suffering due to negativity is a choice we make. Why? Because we often fail to manage our reactions to negativity effectively, allowing it to take over our lives and disrupt our happiness. It's perfectly reasonable to dislike your job due to unfair hours, low pay, or a difficult boss. This is a justifiable form of negativity or struggle because it's a logical response. But if you make no effort to find a better job, set boundaries at work, or improve your sleep habits, and start each day in a bad mood, your suffering becomes self-inflicted.

You have the option to incorporate morning meditation into your routine before heading to work. You can say no to extra work hours when they encroach on your family time or well-being. You can choose to focus on the positive aspects of your job, like having employment, food, and a place to call home, instead of dwelling on the negatives. Granted, it's not always easy, and some people may not be in a financial position to stand up to their bosses or decline extra work. Nevertheless, even in challenging circumstances, you can be kind to yourself by ensuring you get adequate rest and acknowledging your hard work. You can actively seek better job opportunities. If you're not taking any of these steps, you're essentially prioritizing your own misery, thus intensifying it.

Other ways to manage your suffering include seeking support from others, reaching out to a professional to help you navigate loss or distress, or altering your circumstances to facilitate recovery. While not always feasible, changing your mindset remains an option, even when other changes aren't possible.

Managing Your Mental Health

As we delve into the subject of managing circumstances beyond our control, I'd like to shift our focus away from adopting a negative mindset and instead emphasize the significance of addressing an issue of utmost importance: mental illness. I began this book by highlighting that mental disorders have become a widespread affliction, akin to the impact of wars and epidemics on previous generations, yet they remain profoundly misunderstood. So, what exactly constitutes a mental illness, and how does it differ from a negative mindset?

While there exist numerous varieties of mental illnesses, it would be impractical to discuss them all comprehensively. In simple terms, a mental illness is a condition that disrupts, modifies or otherwise influences a person's cognitive processes, behavior, and emotions, going beyond their conscious control and straying from what is considered typical. For instance, premenstrual syndrome (PMS), recognized for causing severe mood fluctuations in women prior to menstruation, does not qualify as a mental disorder. Although their behavior undergoes changes during this time, it stems from the natural hormonal fluctuations inherent in women of childbearing age and is not linked to mental disorders.

On the other hand, bipolar disorder, a mental illness, is characterized by extreme and often unpredictable mood or energy swings, ranging from depressive lows to manic highs (Holland, 2018). Individuals with bipolar disorder may pose risks to themselves or others, and the disorder, albeit influenced by various factors, is likely triggered by a chemical imbalance in the individual's neurological system. Bipolarity is not a natural trait of humans and is therefore classified as a disorder.

In these examples, both mental illnesses and negative mindsets affect one's mood and behavior, but only the former qualifies as a disorder. The same principle applies to nervousness before a significant event versus generalized anxiety or panic disorder, as well as sadness, disappointment, or pain resulting from unforeseen events versus clinical depression or hunger due to neglecting meals versus anorexia nervosa, and so forth.

Mental disorders are typically characterized by physiological abnormalities or inefficiencies within an individual's nervous system. While this is not the sole definition, it serves to illustrate the distinction from negativity.

In the case of depression, for instance, individuals may not produce adequate amounts of dopamine, endorphins, serotonin, or oxytocin, or these neurochemicals may not be efficiently transported to their intended destinations, resulting in an insufficient effect. Consequently, those afflicted are predisposed to feelings of dissatisfaction, unhappiness, self-loathing, and other negative emotions, as they are physically unable to experience happiness or positivity in the same way as someone without depression.

Now, it is crucial to address a harsh reality: mental disorders should not be used as an excuse for toxic behavior towards others. If you suspect that your negativity may be symptomatic of a more severe issue, it is your responsibility to seek the necessary assistance. While mental illnesses may not always be curable, they can be managed. We are fortunate to live in an era marked by remarkable advancements in medicine, providing various options suitable for individuals in diverse circumstances. These options include therapy, medication, rehabilitation, and in some cases, lifestyle changes that can make a substantial difference.

Prioritizing your mental well-being is a fundamental aspect of self-care. If you are aware of the disorders you are grappling with and have taken no steps to address them, you are essentially prolonging your own suffering. To reiterate, there is no shame in not feeling okay, and as society becomes more accepting of mental disorders, the associated stigmas are gradually diminishing. Nevertheless, it remains your responsibility to take the necessary measures to embark on your journey to recovery because, ultimately, you are the only one who can do so. Sometimes, your mindset cannot be changed, and it's important to understand that help is available.

Unforeseen Circumstances

To conclude this chapter, which, ironically, had a rather pessimistic tone, I'd like to discuss those moments when no amount of determination, optimism, self-improvement, or even medication can provide assistance. Life will inevitably throw unexpected challenges your way, and there will be instances where you cannot evade them. Misfortunes, tragedies, and stress are inherent aspects of existence. Loss, humiliation, suffering, fear, heartache, anger, and the full spectrum of negative emotions will be part of your journey. It's crucial to acknowledge that during these times, negativity is entirely justified, anticipated, and a healthy response—your only option will be to experience it.

Nevertheless, don't wait for life to upend itself and then merely accept it because you believe there's nothing you can do. Prepare yourself. Learn to confront negativity in a natural and constructive manner. Establish an emergency plan and ensure you have people, including anonymous online acquaintances, you can lean on when navigating the darkest moments. Additionally, familiarize yourself with embracing the darkness; it's as integral as daylight. Resisting it will only burden you with unnecessary suffering.

There's a saying I often refer to: "Hope for the best but be ready for the worst." Live your life to the fullest, appreciating the present moment (mindfulness can greatly assist in this endeavor). Tomorrow, everything could change, and if you're not prepared, an unexpected challenge could knock you off balance. How can you achieve this preparedness? By fortifying your mental resilience so that it doesn't falter when the world does. It's equally crucial to remember that even when adversity strikes, you remain responsible for yourself. Continue to care for your well-being, and once the initial shock subsides, make an effort to heal. No one enjoys contemplating worst-case scenarios, but one undeniable truth is that life progresses, whether we welcome it or not. Strive to make this progression as painless as possible.

Lesson Learned

Constantly striving for unending positivity is both unnatural and detrimental to your well-being, so avoid the pursuit of perpetual happiness. Such an endeavor reflects arrested emotional growth and has the potential to trigger mood, psychological, or behavioral disorders. Although negativity may not be enjoyable, it can have its uses. The key lies in distinguishing when negativity is essential and suitable versus when it becomes perilous. Even during the most challenging moments, and there will inevitably be moments of profound adversity, your mindset remains significant, and there's no necessity to endure unnecessary suffering.

Chapter 6: Discipline

Let's veer away from the gloomy topics and return to exploring how you can reduce your tendency to be overly negative. Perhaps you didn't take my words seriously before, but cultivating a positive outlook isn't an instantaneous transformation. You won't wake up with a positive mindset one day, and if you don't turn it into a habit, your positivity will slip away. Everyone encounters highs in their mood, moments of happiness, and optimism when life seems fantastic. However, there are also lows, and we often tell ourselves that life is an unpredictable rollercoaster. What a load of nonsense.

Indeed, life is full of surprises, and change is its only constant. That's precisely why it's crucial to establish a sense of stability for yourself. If you manage to do that, when life throws unexpected challenges your way, you won't be easily shaken, and you won't abandon your commitment to staying positive at the first sign of adversity.

Much like every other aspect of fostering positivity, creating stability is easier said than done. You might be wondering how to put any of these recommendations into practice. Countless factors in life can hinder your efforts. Let's consider exercise as an example. You know you should engage in it, maybe you even want to, but when it comes down to it, you lack the time, energy, motivation, and possibly even the space or resources. Exercise is undeniably important, but in your daily life, it may not feel urgent. Your bills, family responsibilities, and various errands demand your attention, and I understand that.

Your children, your job, your home, your social life, grocery shopping, relaxation time – all these are undeniably important. No one is disputing that. However, your health and happiness are just as significant, and if you've relegated them to the backburner, it's a cause for concern.

That's precisely why I've saved this chapter for later. If I had discussed it earlier, I'm almost certain you would have abandoned this book in pursuit of one that caters to your inclination for laziness, procrastination, and excuses. Because, let's face it, you're finding ways to evade the truth, using other aspects of your life as justifications.

This chapter will be the most challenging step because only you can make it happen. So far, I've told you what needs to be done, but not how to go about it. Everything we've covered thus far – health, attitude, decluttering, self-improvement, and self-management – all of it amounts to nothing without one critical attribute.

Discipline

Enough with the excuses; I can sense your resistance through these pages. You might be saying to yourself, "Well, I lack discipline, so forget this, I'm giving up." I won't accept that excuse.

No one, I mean absolutely no one, is born with discipline. It's something we acquire and, surprise, surprise, commit to. Reflect on some of the things you've abandoned or failed to achieve over the years. Was the universe truly conspiring against you, or were you simply lacking in motivation? It's never too late to change your approach to determination, work ethic, or commitment. Pay close attention here because this aspect can either make or break your journey towards a more positive mindset.

The Real Magic

My issue with many self-help books is that they often prioritize validation and superficial rewards over making a genuine impact on people's lives. Consider other books centered around positive thinking; they provide guidance on what to think but neglect to teach you how to think independently or critically. Consequently, you might read such books with the hope of witnessing a miraculous transformation, but in reality, you merely replicate someone else's answers without understanding the underlying principles. Don't misunderstand me; the self-help industry is valuable and can indeed uplift and inspire individuals, leading to life-changing experiences. However, it appears to be saturated with individuals who lack sincerity, causing much of the content produced to resemble empty reassurances like telling someone, "You can win this battle, I believe in you!" and then sending them to the frontlines ill-equipped, devoid of knowledge, weapons, or protection.

Here's the unvarnished truth: none of the techniques or practices I've introduced to you will yield any results unless you possess discipline. These methods are akin to habits; you must diligently and consistently practice them; otherwise, they are futile, mere placeholders you engage in when seeking a quick self-esteem boost without investing genuine effort.

The self-help industry has propagated a misleading notion that transforming your life is a simple task. However, it's not life that changes; it's you. Regardless of how many books on positivity you consume, if you approach them with the same mindset as when you started, you won't witness any significant changes.

The only magic involved in self-improvement is making the conscious decision to change and then following through with unwavering commitment. It means declaring your intent to exercise regularly and consistently, and actually doing so without fail. It entails vowing to cease self-deprecating thoughts and catching yourself when they arise until it becomes second nature.

Much like how you compel yourself to work when you lack motivation or dedicate time and effort to acquiring a new skill, you must practice positivity every single day. Failing to do so will cause it to wither away.

That is the solitary key to success—nothing more, nothing less. There are no enchanting spells, no essential rituals you must perform each morning to appease the gods of good fortune. There are no instruction manuals or success recipes adaptable to your preferred diet. Successful individuals are, fundamentally, disciplined individuals. Period.

Excuses, Excuses

I acknowledge that maintaining discipline can be challenging, which is why many individuals struggle with it. It requires a significant amount of energy, patience, and, notably, willpower, a quality that doesn't come naturally to many of us. There are various factors contributing to the loss of motivation in people. For instance, individuals grappling with depression or anxiety often witness changes in their behavior, and in such cases, discipline is often the first casualty. Simple tasks like taking a shower or checking one's mail can become insurmountable challenges.

These situations are comprehensible because they are not issues that can be resolved through sheer willpower. Suggesting otherwise would be akin to advising someone to power through a migraine or walk on a broken leg.

However, for everyone else, it frequently boils down to laziness. Here, the concept of invincibility rears its head once more. When we fail due to our own laziness, we are often unwilling to admit that we let ourselves down, attributing our difficulties to external factors. This tendency is particularly pronounced in cases of procrastination, as it is more convenient to validate ourselves in this manner.

So, what distinguishes laziness from procrastination? Laziness manifests as a lack of desire or intention to undertake a task. It occurs when you simply don't feel like doing something, so you don't do it. Procrastination, on the other hand, arises when you have the intention to complete a specific task but actively seek to avoid it because you don't feel like doing it. For instance, if you are supposed to clean your house but opt to stay in bed watching Netflix because you don't want to clean, that's laziness. In the same scenario, if you tell yourself, "I'll do some work, go grocery shopping, call my friend, and delete some emails first… then I'll clean," that's procrastination. Regardless, both hinder the development of discipline.

To shield ourselves from acknowledging that we are our own stumbling blocks, we concoct excuses to rationalize our laziness and procrastination. While most of these excuses are feeble, we are so desperate to cast ourselves as victims rather than culprits of failure that we wholeheartedly believe them.

This negative behavior is counterproductive and will not serve your interests. Among the various steps you can take to enhance your discipline, the initial and crucial one is to cease making excuses for your lapses.

Here's a concise list of excuses you must eliminate as you cultivate a positive mindset:

- "I don't have time." Create the time; it's that straightforward.
- "It's not important." Yes, it is. Unless you don't aspire to self-improvement.
- "I forgot." Utilize reminders and alarms; they exist for this very purpose.
- "I'm too tired." Then do it tomorrow, or better yet, take a short rest and then tackle the task. If you employ this excuse, you are deceiving yourself, and it will not count.
- "I'm not motivated." Discipline doesn't rely on motivation. It's the capacity to fulfill your obligations, whether motivated and inspired or not.
- "I'm not ready." Unless you are referring to not being dressed for the gym or needing a bathroom break before starting a task, this justification is baseless. If you follow this rationale, you will never be prepared. Discipline necessitates a "now-or-never" mentality.
- "I'll do it later." Really? I thought as much.

In essence, if you cannot apply the "power of yet" to your reasons for procrastination, they are merely hollow excuses that should be discarded along with your clutter and negativity.

Work Hard, Play Hard

Would you like to uncover the reason why discipline is the sole key to achieving success? The answer lies in the concept of reaping what you sow. The outcome you attain is directly proportional to the effort you invest. If you only engage in meditation once a year, you will only experience the mental clarity it offers on an annual basis. Similarly, if you only exercise when you're in the mood, you won't achieve the desired physique or enjoy those sought-after endorphins as frequently as you'd like. If your goal is to cultivate a positive mindset but you don't put in the effort to maintain positivity, you'll likely remain entrenched in negativity.

This is why I previously mentioned that individuals driven to succeed don't dwell on present challenges; instead, they keep their focus on the ultimate rewards. Positivity serves as the ultimate reward, underscoring the need for discipline in your pursuit of it.

However, I understand that maintaining discipline can be challenging, and that's where the difficulty arises. Discipline can be draining and may sometimes feel like it's robbing you of immediate joy. Yet, giving in to laziness, procrastination, or short-term indulgence at the expense of hard work will ultimately erode your positivity. Work diligently now so that you can enjoy the benefits later. Push through the initial discomfort, and, like any other habit, discipline will eventually become a source of satisfaction beyond your imagination. I assure you of that.

Stick to Your Guns

I won't push you into the deep end. It would be pointless to ask you to be disciplined without providing guidance. So, regarding the steps we've discussed (including this one, in a somewhat unconventional manner), here's how you can assist yourself in implementing them. Keep in mind that progress may be slow initially, and it's crucial not to let it demoralize you. Promise me you won't give up but instead persevere.

Among all the tools at your disposal, consider these tips as the metaphorical baseball bat. You need to pick it up, figure out how to wield it effectively and use it to overcome challenges. However, as the saying goes, you can lead someone to water, but you can't force them to drink. I'm offering you the baseball bat, but it's up to you to find the motivation to use it, and unfortunately, that's something I can't assist with.

Accountability

Failing becomes more probable when you're not under anyone's scrutiny. To your advantage, share your commitments and progress with others. These individuals can be those you have confidence in or even an online audience on social platforms. They might encompass medical professionals, your significant other, your parents, or even a support network of like-minded individuals on a similar journey.

The reasoning here is quite straightforward. When you announce your intentions to someone, you're more likely to stay true to your word. On the contrary, not doing so could lead to complications, such as disappointment, the need for explanations, or the uncomfortable task of admitting errors (and we've already discussed why humans are averse to that). Conversely, by sharing your plans, you'll experience a sense of accomplishment (or, at the very least, avoid the stress of dealing with the repercussions of failing to follow through).

Furthermore, consider that if you ask someone to hold you accountable and you fall short of your resolutions, you expose yourself to judgment. Nobody relishes being judged. Involving others is an effective means to motivate yourself. You'll be much less inclined to make mistakes if you must answer for your missteps.

Positive Reinforcement

If you aim to establish new routines, it's essential to find the motivation to maintain them. Interpret this advice in your unique way, as there is ample room for creativity. Here are some suggestions:

1. Grant yourself a small reward each time you accomplish your daily tasks.
2. Allow yourself one cheat day for every significant achievement you attain.
3. Reserve leisure and enjoyable activities for after you've completed your responsibilities.
4. Treat yourself to some self-care once you've put in the effort.

Your methods can range from the straightforward, like having a piece of candy after a meditation session, to the more intricate, such as celebrating subscriber milestones with a livestream if you're sharing your journey with an audience. The primary goal is to motivate yourself to work more efficiently and enjoy the benefits sooner.

Don't Contemplate, Act

Utilize the techniques outlined in the first chapter, such as creating schedules or maintaining a bullet journal, but avoid improvisation. Relying on improvisation can easily lead you astray because you'll end up following your whims rather than your necessities. Employ a planner, set alarms, utilize reminders, and maintain calendars to mark your commitments. When the designated time arrives, don't disregard them. Don't overthink; don't dwell on your feelings; simply execute the tasks dictated by your planner. Over time, you'll discover your rhythm.

Push Through It Once More

Let's face it, Discipline isn't enjoyable. It's laborious. You might even despise it, finding it uncomfortable, monotonous, and unpleasant. Nevertheless, you must persevere. That's the essence of discipline – compelling yourself to fulfill your obligations, even when you find no joy in it.

However, I must offer a word of caution: be aware of your limits. There's a distinction between discipline and peril. Never push through an injury, a mental health condition, or burnout. Doing so could worsen your situation, so it's essential to discern when it's time to work and when it's time to rest. If you can't identify any underlying issues or valid reasons to avoid exertion, then simply go ahead and do it. Your displeasure won't be eternal, I assure you.

Learned from Experience

Developing a positive mindset isn't an overnight process. It requires you to face the challenge head-on and compel yourself to cultivate it, using the only effective strategy available: discipline.

This skill necessitates practice and refinement. Excuses won't lead to progress, so discard them and invest your efforts in acquiring this skill instead.

Chapter 7: Celebrate Yourself

I've been quite tough on you, haven't I? But now, you can relax because the challenging part is over. From this point forward, I intend to shower you with nothing but admiration and applause, and you truly deserve it. Before we dive into celebrating how incredibly amazing you are, there's one last crucial aspect of positivity that you need to grasp.

Positivity is something that originates from within.

I understand that I've dedicated numerous pages to explaining how it's not something you stumble upon but rather something you actively foster. That concept still holds true. When you make a conscious effort to enhance yourself, you become the architect of your own happiness. So, here's the ultimate truth, one that surpasses all others.

When you commit to exercise for those delightful endorphins or for your desired appearance, weight, or state of being, you're taking control of your own destiny and shaping a positive mindset. The same applies when you train yourself to think more positively, speak kindly, show consideration for others, and maintain order in your life. In fact, if you've been grappling with negativity or have uncovered aspects of yourself that you're not particularly fond of, you embarked on your own journey toward positivity the moment you chose to seek guidance and explore the wisdom contained within this book. I've emphasized numerous times that positivity is a gradual process, and your mindset won't transform overnight. That's a fact. However, the truth remains that you initiated your journey before I imparted any knowledge because you made the conscious decision to seek guidance and learn how to evolve.

Do you know what I believe about this? I find it to be a brilliant and commendable choice. I believe in giving credit where credit is due, and you are owed a substantial amount. I don't take this lightly. The final step in embracing more positivity is to acknowledge and celebrate your progress. This practice of acknowledging your achievements is just as vital as the rest of the journey. It completes the circle, so I urge you not to overlook it, alright?

You might view it as trivial, but remember, positivity starts and ends with you. I don't want to sound clichéd, but you are truly deserving. It's high time you recognized that and took steps to cherish yourself for all the wonderful, influential, and delightful qualities that make you who you are.

Who's a Good Human? You are. I mean that.

Isn't it peculiar how we readily commend others and even the most trivial accomplishments, yet we seldom extend the same acknowledgment to ourselves?

You're familiar with the scenario, right? A young child approaches you and exclaims, "Hey, look at me!" and then proceeds to stand there, not doing anything at all. What do you do? You respond with enthusiasm. You offer applause, or you say, "That's impressive!" or "Well done!" Perhaps you even throw in a high-five. You tell your pet cat it's fantastic, even though it might claw your face off if you keeled over in front of it with no one around to intervene. You reassure your dog that he's a good boy, even when he's done absolutely nothing. My point is, I want you to extend that same kindness to yourself. Celebrate your achievements, no matter how trivial they may seem.

It's uplifting, and it will uplift you, albeit you may feel a tad absurd. But there's nothing wrong with a bit of silliness. It's a positive and amusing quality, so I fail to see any downside here. It's a win-win situation. So go ahead, and pat yourself on the back for winning twice as well.

Setting silliness aside, you might not be aware of how much you accomplish every day, especially when negativity tries to ensnare you. So you didn't conquer the world. You didn't experience joy fix every aspect of yourself or fulfill that promise you made to yourself. But do you know what you did? You opened your eyes this morning. You kept breathing. You battled through your negativity to go to work, cook dinner for your family, or even read this book with the hope of leading a happier life. You did your best, even if your best was just staying awake and facing another day.

That's what admirable humans do. You're still here, hanging on. You're in a state of learning, growth, and transformation. And I find that truly remarkable. This is precisely what I mean when I urge you to acknowledge your worth. Stop relegating yourself to the background and recognize all that you've accomplished to be where you are. Human existence can be challenging at times, and the fact that you haven't given up yet, choosing instead to improve your circumstances, demonstrates that you are a genuine warrior. Or a rock star. Whichever you find cooler!

I've previously discussed the concept of positive reinforcement through the promise of incentives, so I won't dwell on it extensively here. I simply want to clarify that this same principle can also be applied in different contexts beyond disciplinary measures.

Take a moment to appreciate yourself when you achieve something impressive, kind, or remarkable. Acknowledge your own beauty when you genuinely feel it. Create a nickname for yourself based on your strengths, enabling you to showcase them when meeting new people. It may seem a bit unconventional, but it can be effective. The key is to consistently remind yourself of your remarkable qualities and reward yourself for them, not just for your efforts. After all, life shouldn't be all work and no play, right?

The only caveat is to ensure that you don't overindulge in self-reward outside of your commitments, as excessive self-bribery in other areas may diminish its impact within those commitments. So, exercise caution but also enjoy the process!

Toot Your Own Horn

You may want to revisit the section on building confidence because what you're about to do is proudly showcase your assets. This can encompass anything you cherish, whether it's a piece of art you've crafted, a song you love performing, your perspective on a topic, or even the superficial aspects like your appearance or a fancy photograph of your meal.

Often, we restrain ourselves out of fear of criticism. I encourage you to break free from this pattern and replace it with a much healthier one: embracing and celebrating your true self.

There's just one condition to keep in mind - you should only celebrate when it's an expression of self-love. Avoid using this as a pretext for arrogance, toxicity, condescension, or other negative behaviors. Doing so would undermine the purpose of fostering a positive mindset that endures.

Keep in mind that while confidence and self-esteem are distinct, they are commonly seen as interconnected. Nurturing one tends to bolster the other. So, when you proudly showcase what you hold dear, pay attention to how it makes you feel. This will encourage you to do it more frequently, and eventually, confidence will become second nature, and there will be no need for pretense.

Start with small steps if necessary, but occasionally highlighting your own accomplishments is a wonderful way to acknowledge yourself, so seize these opportunities when they arise. Just be mindful not to overdo it.

Lastly, adhere to one more rule here: Be confident on your own terms. Don't flaunt what you think will please others. Flaunt what genuinely makes you proud.

Put Yourself Out There

Perhaps you believe that if you had someone to showcase your talents to, you'd be more inclined to display what you have to offer. This predicament resonates with many individuals. Loneliness and seclusion can dampen one's spirits and lead to a decline in self-assurance or the desire for it.

Here's a suggestion: seek out individuals who will cheer you on. This is an enjoyable method to present your best self, even when you're surrounded by those who care about you.

If you're not yet prepared to put yourself in the spotlight, consider starting a YouTube channel, podcast, or something as straightforward as a blog or a Facebook page. Initially, it may feel intimidating because there's a chance that no one will pay attention or that trolls might emerge with hurtful comments about your work.

However, there are some factors to ponder that can help you overcome these fears. Firstly, even if nobody finds your content engaging, you will know that you had the bravery to give it a shot. This is something that a) not many people have the courage to do, and b) will boost your confidence. Secondly, trolls aren't the only individuals out there. There are also kind-hearted people who will offer support, encouragement, or relate to your experiences. Almost nobody who gained a substantial following began with millions of followers; they had to navigate the same awkward process of finding their footing and battling feelings of inadequacy. Even the most beloved figures on Earth began their journeys unnoticed, with very few exceptions. Lastly, remember that if you don't enjoy it, you have the option to quit at any time. You can delete your videos, podcasts, or social media accounts. This is simply an experiment to determine if it suits you. All you really need is your phone and any ideas you may have, even if you choose to share the story of how you're combating negativity. Dip your toes in the water; you might find it's just the right temperature.

Be Your Own Cheerleader

When it comes to celebrating yourself, I want to emphasize the importance of the word 'yourself.' I understand better than anyone what it's like to feel unsupported, making it seem foolish to be your own advocate. Don't fall for that trap. It's just your self-esteem playing tricks on you, as it tends to exaggerate the consequences of not being liked by others (it imagines you facing a saber-toothed tiger if people don't approve of you). Don't give in to those thoughts; your self-esteem often doesn't have a clue.

However, here's the key point: Even if no one else is cheering you on, remember that it's still your life, your journey, and your corner. So, stand up for yourself. Celebrate not only your major achievements but also your small victories. Believe in yourself, even if others do too. You are just as important as anyone else, so treat yourself with the same consideration. What's holding you back? Seriously, ask yourself that question.

I'm a big advocate of the DIY (Do It Yourself) approach. Support yourself. Acknowledge your accomplishments. March to the beat of your own drum and proudly display your own banner.

Having supporters is undoubtedly a wonderful feeling, and I won't deny the significance of interactions, affection, and encouragement from others. It provides a significant confidence boost because it validates our sense of self-worth. When others recognize it too, it feels substantial, doesn't it?

But have you ever considered that validation presupposes something already exists? You are cool (or strong, or brave, or smart, or beautiful, or whatever suits you). You don't require external validation for that. It's fantastic when it happens, but it's an echo.

So, the ultimate challenge in cultivating positivity is learning to see yourself through the lens of others. What can I say? It's a magnificent perspective.

Lesson Learned

Recognize and celebrate the admirable qualities you already possess. Even if there's no one else to acknowledge them, you can step in and be your own cheerleader, as nothing in this world should hinder you from supporting yourself.

Esteeming yourself may prove to be the most challenging step, but with persistent effort, you'll develop a routine of self-worth, self-love, and confidence. Over time, your self-esteem will rise, and maintaining a positive mindset (which will sustain your progress in these steps) will gradually become an authentic part of your nature, naturally making you a positive individual.

Conclusion

Take a moment to savor your triumph over negativity! Your journey has been nothing short of remarkable, so let's recap how you've masterfully combated pessimism.

First and foremost, you've acknowledged the profound connection between a healthy body and a healthy mind. The wisdom of experts—doctors, scientists, motivational speakers, life coaches, mentors, gurus, and health enthusiasts—has proven true in emphasizing the importance of self-care.

You've also come to recognize that at times, you've been overly critical of yourself due to ingrained programming. Elevating your self-esteem, confidence, and, consequently, your self-worth is both attainable and challenging. It's as simple as not allowing others' opinions to dictate your self-perception. Hopefully, you've cultivated a deeper appreciation for yourself along this transformative journey.

Next, you've grasped the significance of purging negativity from your life. On occasion, you've been your own worst adversary, and we've delved into significant matters such as recognizing your own self-deception and making a firm commitment to adjusting your attitude and your treatment of others.

Subsequently, you've explored the notion that negativity isn't always detrimental and that perpetual happiness isn't a realistic expectation. We've delved into the realm of mental health and how to prepare ourselves for life's unexpected challenges.

Throughout, I've repeatedly emphasized the pivotal role of discipline in your pursuit of positivity. Without it, the task of resetting your mindset and achieving lasting change becomes a daunting challenge.

Lastly, we've celebrated your achievements because, ultimately, you are in control of your destiny. You've conjured your own magic by embarking on this journey to nurture positivity.

Positivity possesses an extraordinary transformative power capable of revolutionizing your life in unimaginable ways. This is not an unfounded claim; it's a well-documented fact observed countless times across different people, situations, and circumstances. While I've strived to demonstrate that there's no secret to positivity, its inherently magical nature has never been disputed. It possesses genuine transformative power, inspiring change. Positivity can be your driving force, reducing your fear of the unknown and boosting your confidence in your chosen path.

A positive mindset can elevate your relationships, lifestyle, and career. You will experience an enhanced sense of self-worth and a brighter outlook on the world, no longer relying on external circumstances for hope, joy, love, confidence, or enthusiasm. Instead, you will radiate your own light, possibly the most brilliant light you've ever encountered, erasing darkness so effectively that you'll forget it ever existed.

This book may have defied your expectations, but that was the intention all along. With "F*ck Your Negative Thoughts," my goal was for you to truly master the art of dismissing negativity—giving it the finger, or two if you prefer. The techniques I've shared with you may not be all about rainbows and sunshine, but rest assured, they will work for you.

I hope I've succeeded in conveying that your life and your mindset are entirely within your control. It all comes down to the materials you use to build it. Positivity serves as the foundational cornerstone upon which your desired happy life can stand tall. Strengthen it, and the storms and unexpected challenges that come your way won't stand a chance of toppling you. And even if, by some unlikely turn of events, they do manage to knock you down, you now possess the knowledge to stand back up. There may be some wrinkles to iron out, but your resilient mind can handle it.

Your journey has been intense, and I wouldn't be surprised if you're relieved to reach the end. Don't forget to celebrate. Completing this book is a small but significant victory. So, go ahead, and reward yourself. When you're finished, there's just one more thing I ask of you: go out there and conquer those sour lemons that life has thrown your way.

I believe in your ability to do it. Now, I hope you do too.